PROCESS CATHOLICISM

An Exercise in Ecclesial Imagination

Robert L. Kinast

University Press of America,® Inc.
Lanham • New York • Oxford

Copyright © 1999 by
University Press of America,® Inc.
4720 Boston Way
Lanham, Maryland 20706

12 Hid's Copse Rd.
Cumnor Hill, Oxford OX2 9JJ

Library of Congress Cataloging-in-Publication Data

Kinast, Robert L.
Process Catholicism : an exercise in ecclesial imagination / Robert L.
Kinast.
p.   cm.
Includes bibliographical references.
1. Catholic Church—Doctrines. 2. Process theology. Title.
BX1751.2.K53 1999   230'.2—dc21   98-54387 CIP

ISBN 0-7618-1339-X (cloth: alk. ppr.)
ISBN 0-7618-1340-3 (pbk: alk. ppr.)

⊖™ The paper used in this publication meets the minimum
requirements of American National Standard for Information
Sciences—Permanence of Paper for Printed Library Materials,
ANSI Z39.48—1984

In tribute to

Cardinal Joseph Bernardin
whose love for the church
sustained my own for thirty years

and

Michael A. Morris
whose friendship, wit, and courage
always put things in perspective

Contents

Preface

It's not easy being a Catholic at the end of this century. Perhaps it has never been easy. Certainly when I was growing up in Pittsburgh in the 1940s and '50s, I constantly heard my parents, relatives, teachers, clergy, and other church authorities tell me that it was hard being a good Catholic (they always added "good" to distinguish real Catholics from those who just went through the motions).   Even my non-Catholic friends somewhat admiringly admitted that it was hard being a Catholic. And it was, but it was hard for the wrong reasons.

We were expected to affirm and defend, even if we didn't understand, doctrines which other Christians did not profess (the infallibility of the pope, the immaculate conception and bodily assumption of Mary, the transubstantiation of bread and wine at Mass). We were expected to carry out certain practices which other Christians did not (worship in a language few understood, abstinence from meat on Friday and from food and drink before Communion, Lenten sacrifices, year-round offering up of unpleasant things, praying for the poor souls in purgatory, saying the rosary--even watching Bishop Sheen on television).

All of these things clearly distinguished us as Catholics but few of them were essential to the faith. What was important was that we said and did what Catholics were supposed to say and do. The meaningfulness of everything was taken for granted, or not taken into account at all. This is what really made it difficult to be a Catholic and why many of my peers, as they matured, decided the church was childish, irrelevant, and unnecessary in their lives.

Then came Vatican II. Contrary to conventional assessments at that time, and even today, the council did not make it easy to be a Catholic. It made it difficult, but for the right reasons. Vatican II reasserted what was central to the Christian faith and challenged us to claim it as our own: fidelity to the Jesus of the gospels while living fully engaged in the modern world. By comparison, mastering obscure teachings and perpetuating unusual practices seemed gleefully easy.

In retrospect what Vatican II did was issue a call to conversion for the church as a whole. Unlike previous councils, this was not a call to conversion from immorality to morality or from heresy to orthodoxy. It was a conversion to a new way of being Catholic (and for the right reasons). In this respect it was very much like the conversion appeal of Jesus, as recorded in the canonical gospels. His summons was not necessarily to a conversion from immorality to morality. In fact, Jesus repudiated the facile assumption that people were immoral because they had a physical handicap, were of low social status, or of female gender. Nor did he preach a conversion from heresy to orthodoxy. Jesus seemed content to let the experts argue the nuances of the Torah—although when he was accused of distorting its meaning, he was willing to enter into debate and explain his interpretations.

The real conversion which Jesus proclaimed was a new way of being Jewish. It was not just a change in this or that belief or practice; it was a wholesale change in the people's orientation to life. The basis for this conversion was a startling image--that of God reigning joyously and immediately in the everyday lives of all the people. Everything Jesus said and did was intended to bring people to the point of recognizing this reigning presence of an intimate God and to respond to it with all their heart and mind and soul.

Jesus offered no systematic doctrine, no catechism or encyclopedia, no rival rabbinical school of interpretation. He did not establish a program of spiritual exercises for achieving the desired changes. He took whatever situation presented itself, saw its possibilities for conversion, tried to enact them, and then added that bit of insight to the meaning of God-reigning. How does Vatican II parallel the example of Jesus?

Although the council had a defined agenda and produced sixteen separate documents, it constantly addressed the nature of the church itself and thereby touched upon everything pertaining to it. Just as important, Vatican II addressed the nature of the church imaginatively, describing it in as many creative ways as possible, beginning with the rich stream of images in no. 6 of the Constitution on the Church. In this respect Vatican II was an exercise in ecclesial imagination.

After nearly forty years of involvement with the council as a seminary student, parish priest, diocesan official, and theologian, I sense a greater need than ever for ecclesial imagination to sustain and advance the initiative of Vatican II. And encouragingly such ecclesial imagination is being displayed in many places. There are missionaries who have taken seriously the meaning of inculturation and are trying to be Christian companions to the religious flourishing of native peoples; there are theologians who have been pressing for unprecedented dialogue with representatives of other religions, generating a new comparative theology; there are communities of faith who value their own experience as a source of theology and are creating contextual, *mestizo*, womanist, boundary, and marginal theologies.

This same spirit has brought new respect to neglected members of the church, especially the poor and women, honoring them as sources of religious practice and theological insight for the whole church. In the first instance it has led to a preferential option for the poor, if not yet a church of the poor; in the second instance it has led to a new appreciation of feminine experience, if not yet a church of true equals. In both instances people are claiming the integrity of their experience and using it to construct a new way of being Catholic.

These are exciting, unprecedented exercises of ecclesial imagination, but they are being increasingly inhibited as the church moves toward the end of this century. There is a growing preoccupation with conceptual precision (in the form of concise answers), dogmatic orthodoxy (in the form of right answers), and intellectual conformity (in the form of answers only). Too much of this mentality squeezes the environment of the church and stifles its imagination. As a result, it is once again becoming hard to be a Catholic, and once again for the wrong reasons. For those of us who lived through the exhilarating aftermath of Vatican II, it would be a cruel betrayal of the council to re-institute the mentality which Vatican

II rejected. On the other hand, it would be a fitting testimony to the council to continue exercising the ecclesial imagination it promoted. That is the intent of this book. It is an exercise of ecclesial imagination--in this case with the help of the process philosophy of Alfred North Whitehead. Hence the title of the book, *Process Catholicism*. Why use process philosophy? On a personal level, I am a process theologian and I find that a process worldview is a stimulating way to think through most topics, including ecclesiology. Second, and more importantly, I find that a great many Catholics, at least in the U.S., share the basic outlook of process thought (which will be described in chapters two and three). This is not surprising because the main architects of process thought have been Americans, or in the case of Whitehead, a thinker steeped in British empiricism who spent the latter years of his life in the U.S.

The third reason for using process thought is that I believe in the value of an imaginative attitude toward the church. I don't think there can be too many creative, speculative, stimulating ways of approaching the mystery which is church. As Vatican II energetically demonstrated, no single metaphor or system of thought can adequately grasp this mystery. And as Whitehead cautioned in another context, we should be more wary of a celibacy of the mind than an indulgence in imagination.

Of course, it remains to be seen whether process thought can supply a sufficiently imaginative and revealing view of the church. It does for me and I hope it will for you. But even if it doesn't, there is still a constant need for ecclesial imagination, especially as we enter the next millennium. For we are made in the image of God, and we are never more like the image of God than when we exercise our imagination.

Acknowledgments

This book has been in process for more than five years, longer than any other book I have written. It began with the lure of a title, *Process Catholicism*, which I was intrigued to explore and unpack. In part I wanted to think through what a process worldview might contribute to ecclesiology; in part I wanted to find a fresh perspective for understanding and dealing with the struggles of the Catholic church in the post-Vatican II era. In no way did I anticipate how difficult and time-consuming this project would become.

Along the way there were many times when I was not sure what I was trying to accomplish, whether I was able to achieve it, and what value it would have if I succeeded. It would have been very easy to abandon the effort altogether, except for certain individuals who kept me motivated, informed, and encouraged. I want to acknowledge them now with deep and lasting gratitude.

Joseph Bracken has been a friend and colleague in process studies for many years. He believed in this project from the time I first mentioned it to him. More than that, he carefully read my several versions of the formal process material, offering insight, clarification, and critique that have been immensely helpful. Most of all, he has offered constant encouragement and support for what I have attempted to do. His influence is everywhere in the book, even if he is cited on only certain pages.

John Cockayne is a loyal friend and dedicated parish priest who never failed to ask how my process ecclesiology was coming along when he would call for a "catch-up chat." He eagerly read most sections of the manuscript and invariably indicated how much this way of thinking was needed on the pastoral level. His enthusiasm was too persuasive to let me abandon this task.

John Cobb has not only enlightened me (and so many others) through his elaboration of process theology, but he also extended a timely and gracious endorsement of this project. When I told him I was having difficulty finding a publisher, he asked for a manuscript copy of the book so the Center for Process Studies would be sure to have it in its collection no matter what else happened. Not long afterwards, the University Press of America agreed to publish *Process Catholicism*.

Others have contributed in ways they may not have realized: Bernard Lee for his helpful and honest suggestions about situating this study experientially, Larry Boadt at Paulist Press for affirming that I was addressing a real conundrum in the church (albeit in controversial terms), Hal Rast at Trinity Press for complimenting my explanation of Whitehead's thought as both substantial and intelligible, numerous colleagues who always responded positively when I described the purpose of this book, and members of my family who listened patiently and appreciatively when I tried to explain what I was writing about.

Of course, at the center of this project is Judith, as she is at the center of everything I do and am. Her usual buoyant support for anything I decide to do was challenged this time by my many detours and dead ends, but typically she found both the reasons and the resources to get me back on track. I am not only grateful to her but constantly amazed that when I finally put my original inspiration into words, she has already known it all along—and much, much more besides.

Chapter 1

The Church At Present:
Confronting Pastoral Heresy

The Catholic church in the U.S. is currently struggling with a number of pastoral heresies.

Despite official statements proclaiming the equality of women with men, the male experience and way of doing things in the church functions as the standard which women are "equal to," with the result that women are still expected to act as men think they should.

Despite official affirmations of the value of inculturation, the European-American experience of the faith functions as the norm to be preserved by every other cultural expression, with the result that minority groups remain subordinate to and measured by the "Euro-tradition."

Despite unprecedented opportunities for lay leadership at every level of the church, including Sunday worship and the permanent deaconate for men, the ministerial priesthood with its current requirements for ordination functions as the priority, with the result that whole communities of the faithful are denied the celebration of Sunday Eucharist.

Despite the proliferation of small faith communities and testimony concerning the quality of experience within them, the territorial parish functions as the indispensable structure with which small faith communities are expected to affiliate for their validity, with the result that alternative forms of organization are perceived as a threat to, if not an aberration of, traditional Catholic life.

Despite the key role of professional theologians at Vatican II and the importance of their competence in a pluralistic, ever-expanding information age, the hierarchy functions as the only authentic magisterium in the church, with the result that theologians are given the role of explaining the teachings of the episcopal magisterium and keeping their own disagreements private.

Despite the resounding endorsement by Vatican II of the modern ecumenical movement, the Catholic tradition functions as the sole norm of authenticity with the result that the Protestant experience of faith is still treated as inferior, deficient, and not able to contribute much to the Catholic church.

What does it mean to call these situations pastoral heresies? After all, the term heresy is usually reserved for doctrinal disputes, where it means the obstinate denial by a baptized person of a truth believed to be part of divine, catholic faith.[1] Such a denial usually comes at the end of a much longer and more complex process; a heresy rarely begins as an outright denial of an article of faith. In fact, most heresies have a history of development, corresponding to the related doctrinal development and even contributing to it. In this respect heresy can have a positive role as part of a living faith seeking to understand and clarify itself.[2]

In its best sense a heresy affirms a truth that appears to be undervalued, misconstrued, or neglected. This in itself does not constitute a heresy, of course. Such a corrective affirmation becomes a heresy only when it denies the teaching that is correlative to the point it is attempting to make. Thus affirming the humanity of Jesus becomes a heresy when it effectively denies his divinity (as with Arianism). Likewise, affirming the divinity of Jesus becomes a heresy when it effectively denies his humanity (as with Gnosticism).

At this point the literal meaning of heresy comes into play. It is a deliberate choice (from the Greek, *haeresis*) to affirm a particular truth at the expense of the larger truth to which it belongs, as that truth is known and proclaimed by the church as a whole. The motives for making such a choice will vary with each individual or group and are notoriously difficult to judge accurately. More important, they are not nearly as enlightening as are the conditions which make heresy both possible and inevitable.

Christian faith is positioned between contrasting truths such as the omnipotence of God and the autonomy of creation, the divine will and human freedom, the experience of God as transcendent and as immanent, divine revelation and human reason, grace and free will, immortality and death. In attempting to honor each pair adequately (without ever knowing either of them completely), human beings will undervalue, misconstrue, or neglect essential truths. This will happen even when people are sincerely trying to understand and express the truth because each of the pairs is exceedingly complex and intertwined with all the others. For this reason there is a long-standing distinction between material heresy which denies an essential truth without necessarily intending to do so and formal heresy which knowingly and deliberately denies an essential truth.

Given this brief description of doctrinal heresy, what does pastoral heresy mean? A pastoral heresy is a deliberate choice to structure and carry out the practical life of the church erroneously. It is a denial in practice of how the members of the church should relate to one another. This strikes at the very heart of what it means to be church as a living community of believers. The typical form of pastoral heresy, as indicated by the examples above, is that one member or group in a church relationship claims or assumes the privilege of determining how the whole relationship should be understood, structured, and carried out. This in effect is a denial of the communal nature of the church whereby each member is empowered by the gifts of the Holy Spirit to contribute to a consensus about how members should relate to one another.

Such a heresy is pastoral because it pertains to the way the life of the church is structured and carried out, i.e., to the way the members of the church are expected to interact with one another in constituting the church. In this sense pastoral heresy pertains to church practice but not in the restricted sense of this or that particular activity. Rather pastoral heresy pertains to church practice in a fuller and more original sense, as a way of life learned, shared, and developed by the members of the church together.[3] Obviously specific practices are involved in this understanding of the pastoral life of the church but pastoral heresy refers to the way the experience of being-church is structured rather than to specific shortcomings or disagreements in the enactment of that experience.

Accordingly a heresy is not pastoral simply because a member of the clergy (a pastor) is involved or because it concerns those activities traditionally entrusted to the clergy such as worship, preaching, ministry, and church administration. Likewise a pastoral heresy is not just an occasional erroneous practice (e.g., rebaptizing a convert who is already validly baptized) or the failure (even refusal) to carry out what the church as a whole has decided to do (e.g., include women in the roles of lector and eucharistic minister). These mistaken pastoral practices are often based on ignorance of changes in the church, a preference for habitual ways of doing things, or simple laziness rather than a deliberate choice to act contrary to what the church expects in practice.

Like a doctrinal heresy, a pastoral heresy usually evolves slowly and is not immediately recognized as erroneous. When it does emerge, it embodies a choice which affirms a partial truth (for example, the validity of male experience, the importance of the ordained priesthood for Eucharist) at the expense of a larger truth as understood and practiced by the church as a whole (the equal validity of female experience, the primacy of the Eucharist). Affirming this larger truth should be the goal in confronting pastoral heresy, not attributing motives to those who practice it. In this way a pastoral heresy can help clarify how the church should function in order to be the church at a given time and in a given place. Humanly speaking, however, pastoral heresies like doctrinal heresies tend to foster conflict, polemics, and hostility among the members of the church which makes the search for truth-in-practice more difficult to carry out.

The Search for Common Ground

A striking corroboration that the Catholic church in the U.S. is struggling with pastoral heresy is the Catholic Common Ground Initiative, proposed by Cardinal Joseph Bernardin before his untimely death in 1996. The position paper for this Initiative, "Called to Be Catholic: Church in a Time of Peril," did not use the term pastoral heresy but its description of the Catholic church in the U.S. fits the meaning sketched above.[4]

The statement describes the current experience of Catholics. Its focus is on the way Catholics relate to one another, i.e., their pastoral life, with particular attention to how they communicate with one another. While acknowledging that there are vital communities and efforts to build consensus and cooperation in American Catholicism, the statement bluntly admits that party lines have hardened and a mood of suspicion and acrimony hangs over active members in the church. Constructive debate is supplanted by bickering, disparagement and stalemate as fear and polarization afflict or inhibit the church's discussion of urgent issues. "Rather than forging a consensus that can harness and direct the church's energies, contending viewpoints are in danger of canceling each other out."[5] That assessment is the essence of a pastoral heresy, and the heart of the peril which the church faces.

The proposed solution is for all Catholics to reclaim their common ground of faith, centered on Jesus Christ in Scripture and sacrament, accountable to the whole Catholic tradition, and open to "the full range and demands of authentic unity, acceptable diversity and respectful dialogue...."[6] Indeed dialogue, consultation, and public discussion of differences are the chief means which the Initiative envisions, and has thus far put into practice, to achieve a revitalized Catholic common ground.

Predictably the statement evoked conflicting responses from both hierarchy and laity, exemplifying to some degree the very atmosphere which the statement described. On the whole, however, most Catholics seemed to acknowledge that the Project had identified a serious problem which needs to be addressed constructively. Seeking a common ground through dialogue is certainly one reasonable approach for doing this. But it is not the only approach, and perhaps not the most effective approach for dealing with pastoral heresy.

The Search for New Ground

In responding to the pastoral heresies mentioned above, it is possible to seek, not a common ground, but a new ground. Seeking new ground does not mean starting a new church or reconstituting the existing church with no regard for its self-understanding developed through the ages. Seeking a new ground means imagining "with fresh eyes, open minds, and changed hearts"[7] how the members of the church could actually relate to one another in constituting the church. It is not so much re-gaining or re-vitalizing what has been but projecting and proposing what might be. To do this, it is necessary to exercise ecclesial imagination.

Exercising ecclesial imagination means taking a vantage point that is not already well known and thought out. This introduces fresh perspectives, stimulates creativity, and allows for genuinely new

developments in thought and action. Usually disciplines outside
church life and theology provide the best resources for doing this.
Certainly the social sciences have offered the church a unique
perspective for viewing itself as a social institution. Communications
and systems theory have helped church commentators understand
better the dynamics of decision-making and leadership styles. The use
of models and paradigms in the empirical sciences has given
theologians new ways to analyze and discuss the nature of the church.
Even business and management principles have contributed to the
clarification of the church's mission, objectives, and evaluation
procedures.

The most ancient and congenial partner for this kind of imaginative
theology has been philosophy. Although philosophical worldviews
have rarely been applied directly to ecclesiology, especially at the
pastoral level, nonetheless, I want to seek new ground for overcoming
the pastoral heresies which the church currently faces by using the
philosophy of organism developed by Alfred North Whitehead. Since
his worldview is popularly known as process philosophy, I am calling
this exercise of ecclesial imagination, Process Catholicism. The
groundwork for it is laid out in the next chapter.

Notes

1.   The *Catechism of the Catholic Church*, no. 2089 (Washington, DC:
USCC Office of Publications) 1994.
2.   See Karl Rahner, *On Heresies*, tr. W. J. O'Hara (New York: Herder and
Herder, 1964) 41-67.
3.   This larger sense of practice has been revived in recent years by the
renewal of practical theology and the appreciation of popular religiosity. On
the former, see Thomas Groome, *Sharing Faith* (San Francisco:
HarperCollins) 1991 and Don Browning, *A Fundamental Practical Theology*
(Minneapolis: Fortress Press) 1991. On the latter, see Orlando Espín, *The
Faith of the People: Theological Reflections on Popular Catholicism*
(Maryknoll, NY: Orbis Books) 1997.
4.   See Cardinal Joseph Bernardin/The Common Ground Project, "Called to
Be Catholic: Church in a Time of Peril," *Origins*, 26 (August 29, 1996) 166-
170.
5.   Ibid., 167.
6.   Ibid., 168.
7.   Ibid., 169.

Chapter 2

Seeking New Ground for the Church: A Process Worldview

The philosophy of organism, or process philosophy, is an imaginative understanding of reality which emphasizes the process of becoming (reality-as-event) rather than the nature of being (reality-as-substance). What does this emphasis in process thought have to contribute to an understanding of church? Judging from a survey of the existing literature, it would seem not much. Ecclesiology is not a prominent topic among process theologians.[1] Why is this?

First of all, the majority of process theologians do not belong to the broad catholic tradition (Roman, Orthodox, Anglican) which highlights ecclesiology. Second, most process theologians continue to work on the philosophical agenda set out by Alfred North Whitehead (and his chief successor, Charles Hartshorne). That agenda is concerned with issues such as the nature and knowability of God, the relationship of God to creation and history, the problem of evil, the search for meaning in a contingent world, the correlation of religion with contemporary worldviews—but not the nature of the church. Lastly, process theology has been developed largely in an academic context where the life of the church and related pastoral issues are marginal, if they are discussed at all.[2]

In addition to these factors, Whitehead coined a number of unusual terms to explain his system (prehension, concrescence, superject,

conceptual reversion, panentheism) and he used other, common terms
(such as society, proposition, feeling, occasion) in a technical,
unfamiliar sense. This makes process thought somewhat difficult to
grasp in itself and somewhat awkward to apply directly to ecclesiology
which has its own well-established terminology and agenda. On the
other hand, these very difficulties can provide the challenge needed to
prod the ecclesial imagination in new directions. With this goal in
mind, I want to set forth the main features of Whitehead's worldview
and give a preliminary indication of their relevance for an
understanding of church.[3]

A Dynamic World

The fundamental assertion of a process worldview is that reality is
ultimately composed of dynamic energy events rather than static,
completed objects or substances. This may seem to fly in the face of
everyday perception because we see a world full of real objects like tables
and books and rocks which appear solid and inert. In this instance,
however, appearance is misleading. With the help of modern science,
especially physics, it is now known that all those apparently inert things
are actually, in the final analysis, composed of imperceptible, compact
clusters of energy events.

Whitehead's philosophy of organism was his attempt to explain
philosophically these findings of modern physics. His insistence on the
thoroughly dynamic character of the universe is the reason why
Whitehead's system was called "process" philosophy, although he himself
did not use that term. It points to the constant state of becoming which
characterizes all things. Whitehead expressed this fact as the fundamental
ontological principle of his worldview. It asserts that for anything to be
actual, it must be in the process of its own becoming (e.g., my writing this
book) or an ingredient in the becoming of something else (your reading
what I have written). In contrast to the classic worldview inherited from
the Greeks, Whitehead asserted that to be is to become, and that a thing's
activity (its becoming) constitutes its essence.

Expanding on the last point, Whitehead insisted that each event is also
self-creative, i.e., it determines its own becoming by the way it experiences
itself in relation to its environment. This does not mean that every event in
the universe exercises a conscious, deliberate choice to become one thing
rather than another. It means that the actual existence of each event is
determined by its own experience of itself, not by another entity outside of
it.

The dynamism which characterizes the process world is not mere activity, randomly or arbitrarily happening. Every event comes into being in response to an aim or purpose for its becoming. These aims are supplied by God who in turn draws them out of the events which have immediately preceded the new act of becoming. This process will be explained in more detail later. For the present, it is important to recognize that everything in a process world is engaged in dynamic and purposeful acts of becoming.

How does this dynamic aspect of a process worldview contribute to ecclesial imagination? It prompts the church to imagine itself as an event of continual becoming rather than an ordered body with a fixed nature containing timeless teachings, established practices, and permanent structures. Any element considered part of the essence of the church or constituting its transcendental nature exists by being constantly incorporated into the active life of the church. For example, the Bible would not be thought of primarily as a book with specific contents and objective truths but as an inexhaustible source of experience as it is read and studied and prayed over by the church. The reality of the Bible is constituted by the church's activity with the Bible. The same is true for the sacraments, the creed, and other elements which are typically included in the makeup of the church.[4]

In short, process thought imagines the church to be real insofar as it is engaged in the activity of becoming the church. There is no ecclesial reality apart from the events which constitute the life of the church; there is no timeless, immutable essence existing independent of ecclesial activity. The church is what the church does (to paraphrase Forrest Gump). This view does not eliminate the importance or reality of such things as the Bible, the liturgy, the creed, the hierarchy, the pastoral care, the spirituality, the mission of the church, but it insists on their being understood in a dynamic way, as part of the actual becoming of the church at every moment, as elements constantly shaped by and shaping the experience which is church.

This dynamic view of reality and of church does have a problematic aspect. As mentioned above, the process of becoming which makes everything (including the church) real is self-creative. Being self-creative means that the existence of the church and all its constituent elements are radically dependent on the church's current experience of itself. This experience is the only church which is actually becoming and therefore, according to the ontological principle, the only church which really exists. It is the current experience of church which determines how the past experience of church will be maintained and what value will be given to claims for its transcendent, essential nature.

This does not mean that in each moment the church begins anew, picking and choosing arbitrarily what it will be and how it will be. With the church as with everything else in a process world, the events of the past (including the concrete realizations of ideals) exert a powerful influence on the possibilities for new becoming in the present. This is because the aims for new becoming which initiate every process arise from the events of the past. These events act persuasively on the present to reenact and preserve them into the future. This is what Whitehead called the causal efficacy of the past. Its effectiveness, however, is determined by the self-creative activity of the present.

Process ecclesiology acknowledges the radical contingency of the past on the present and of the transcendent on the existential. This contingency means that the survival and flourishing of the church are not automatically assured apart from the actual becoming of the church from moment to moment. Process ecclesiology does not allow the church to imagine itself being rescued from itself by the intervening hand of an external God. Neither does it encourage a pelagian self-confidence that the church will endure by its own efforts alone. The former denies the self-creativity of process reality; the latter denies that God is involved in the initiation of every act of self-creation.

Process ecclesiology imagines the church at every moment creating itself out of the heritage available to it by including in its experience events from the past and elements from its nature. Inclusion of both does not mean simply finding a place for them the way I look for room on my shelf to store one more book. Inclusion means allowing past events and transcendental elements to contribute actively to the experience of the new event; it means giving them an influential role in the shaping of new occasions. In this way the church's heritage and nature are viewed not as a mute collection of past events and abstract ideals but as a vibrant, appealing source of experience beckoning the church to grasp them and make them part of the next moment of church becoming.

From a process perspective, therefore, Matthew 16: 18 ("upon this rock I will build my church and the gates of the nether world shall not prevail against it") is not a divine guarantee in spite of human freedom and the contingency of history. It is a divine proclamation of confidence in human freedom to discern within the contingency of history how God sees the church becoming and to respond to God's vision with appropriate action.

This self-creative dynamism of process ecclesiology also counteracts a fundamental source of pastoral heresy.

Pastoral heresy typically consists of one person or group claiming the right to determine how the relationships which constitute the church should be defined, structured, and carried out. Ordinarily this claim is based on a source of authority which is assumed to pre-exist or transcend the changing life of the church. Process ecclesiology counteracts this tendency by refusing to grant any structure, tradition, or pattern of activity a real status apart from the actual life of the church. All ecclesial elements belong to the continual becoming of the church; they exist insofar as they are included in the living experience of the church. Therefore no individual, group, or office can claim the right or privilege to determine the pastoral relationships of the church by invoking a separate source of authority or experience. Outside the church there is no ecclesial reality.

This view does not deny the role of leadership and authority in the church, perhaps even as traditionally structured. It does, however, insist on keeping these roles radically contingent on the actual experience of the church's becoming from moment to moment. What this means and how it works in practice should become clearer as the process worldview is explained. For now it can be said that process ecclesiology imagines the church as a dynamic event of constant becoming determined by the self-creative experience of its members. Everything which pertains to church must be understood in terms of this same dynamic character.

An Organic World

In Whitehead's view all self-creative events of becoming form an inclusive, organic whole. This holistic perspective was what Whitehead really wanted to emphasize and the reason why he called his system a philosophy of organism. By this term he wanted to stress two things.

First of all, everything is interconnected in a dynamic way, i.e., the becoming of each event is inherently related to the immediate environment in which it occurs and the immediate environment is shaped by the becoming of each event in its ambit. This dynamic reciprocity between event and environment yields ever larger and more complex connections, extending eventually to the whole universe as one interlocking, organic continuum. Because of the interdependence between event and environment, both are constantly adjusting to the influence and becoming of the other. Therefore, no matter what slice of reality one considers (a family function within a parish, a parish liturgy within a diocese, a diocesan convocation within the universal church) it is a network of influences, impulses, urges, and energy flowing back and forth in multiple directions. In a process world nothing is static and nothing is confined to its own inner point of experience.

Second, the discrete events which make up the organic continuum are distinguished from one another by a difference of degree rather than a difference of essence. This is because the process of becoming is the same for all events. Obviously there are differences between a molecule and a flower, between a rock and a human being, but these differences are due to the type and amount of experience each one can include in its becoming. The process by which each thing senses its aim, experiences itself fulfilling that aim in relation to its environment, and makes its experience available for new acts of becoming is the same. There are no essentially different types of realities in a process world and no exceptions to the universal rules of process.

How does this organic aspect of a process worldview contribute to ecclesial imagination? It stimulates the church to imagine itself as an organic whole being constantly constituted by its interrelated events rather than an organic whole already constituted in its essential fullness. Both views reflect typical "catholic" ecclesiology wherein local churches are concrete expressions of the one organic church which is prior both temporally and theologically. This is in contrast to typical congregational ecclesiology where each congregation is an autonomous church which may or may not choose to join a larger federation of churches. The congregation is no less church if it does not join such a federation and if it does join, it has no essential or necessary connection to other churches.

Both views also express a "catholic" concern for community whereby individuals and groups in the church are bound to one another by real relations and mutual influence. The earliest and most graphic advocate of this organic view of church was St. Paul. His image of the body of Christ and the realistic way he described the union of Christ and members has remained a model for organic ecclesiologies ever since. He gave classic expression to this union when he wrote that if one member suffers, all suffer and if one member rejoices, all rejoice (1 Cor. 12:26). This sentiment certainly fits a process worldview where everything is interconnected and mutually influential.

The difference between the organic character of process ecclesiology and of typical catholic ecclesiology is also the problematic aspect of the former. It is twofold. In process ecclesiology the fullness of the church is what it is at any given moment. It is the sum total of the church's experience of becoming as realized at the present time. Its fullness is not a separate entity kept intact in another order of reality mysteriously shadowing the actual church on earth. In a process world the origin, sustenance, and continuation of the church as an organic whole depends on the self-becoming of the individuals and groups who comprise the church.

Process ecclesiology affirms the organic wholeness of the Catholic church but it is a wholeness which shifts and adjusts from moment to moment in relation to the actual experiences of its members. As a dynamic entity in relationship with other dynamic entities in the world, the content of the church's wholeness is constantly becoming. The church is always the organic whole that it is but this may be more or less whole when compared to the church at another time and in other circumstances. The value of such a comparison is to help the church recognize what its wholeness might be at present, not to reclaim a wholeness which presumably once existed. This understanding of the organic nature of the church has direct implications for ecumenism.

From a process perspective, the goal of ecumenism is not so much to regain a former unity as to experience a present wholeness. The task is not so much to agree on disputed doctrinal formulations or structural requirements from the past but to reach consensus on what it means to become church today and to use the most effective means for putting that consensus into practice. Ecumenical agreements concerning the past are an invaluable resource for reaching consensus about the present but they are not the end result of ecumenism. Indeed the end result of ecumenism (determining what the wholeness of the church might mean in the present) is constantly being redefined and pursued anew. There is no other unity and there is no other wholeness than what the present experience of the church allows.

The second problematic aspect of the organic character of process ecclesiology is that all perceived or claimed differences are a matter of degree, not of essence. There are no essentially different groups in the church (in contrast to Vatican II's claim for the ministerial priesthood in the Constitution on the Church, no. 10) or completely separate realities (in contrast to the council's depiction of the realms of faith and reason in the Pastoral Constitution on the Church in the Modern World, no. 59).

Process ecclesiology certainly acknowledges real differences in the opinions and actions, roles and functions among members of the church and between church members and other people. However, in the ecclesial imagination of process thought these are differences of degree distinguished by how much information or experience one takes into account, how intensely or completely one feels a certain event or relationship, how much importance one attributes to a given teaching, function, custom, or structure. These are real differences and some are more conducive to (or restrictive of) church becoming than others but all of them contribute to the organic wholeness which is the church at any moment.

The primary ecclesial benefit of insisting on degrees of difference rather than differences of essence is that it rejects dualistic, separatist ways of thinking and thereby undercuts one of the chief causes of pastoral heresy. Members of the church who determine unilaterally how a church relationship should be understood, structured, and enacted function as if they are separate from the other members of the relationship and are in a superior position to determine it. This is not necessarily an act of ego gratification. It may also be the consistent carrying out of official responsibilities according to a particular theological understanding, as is the case currently with the official theology of the priesthood in the Catholic church. In any event, a dualistic imagination encourages pastoral heresy whereas the organic perspective of process ecclesiology fosters an ecclesial imagination that prizes the wholeness of the church and the degrees of difference within it.

An Empirical World

The third feature of Whitehead's worldview follows from its dynamic and organic character. Process reality is radically empirical and experiential, i.e., it is grounded in the actual realities and processes of the world as the world lets itself be known. Whitehead himself epitomized this attitude. He certainly engaged in large scale speculation, abstraction, and generalization but always as an explanation of the stubborn facts of the concrete world. His was no detached dogma, spun out logically from hypothetical first principles. His views were always subject to the correction of empirical evidence and actual experience. This constant interplay between facts and interpretation, between observation and reflection, between the particular and the general characterizes not only Whitehead's way of thinking but the nature of a process world as well.

How does the empirical strain of process thought contribute to ecclesial imagination? It challenges the church to temper its speculation and theoretical claims by the facts of its experience and actual existence in contrast to a detached, a-historical description of the church with unverifiable claims and periodic lapses into unintelligibility in the name of mystery. Process ecclesiology trains the church's imagination on the depth and fullness of ecclesial experience, confident that the facts contain enough richness and stimulation to sustain the most imaginative theology the church can generate.

The empirical aspect of a process worldview is very compatible with Jesus' own criteria of verification. When asked by the disciples of John what they should say to their teacher about Jesus, he pointed to the observable effects of his teaching and ministry (LK 7:22-23). In the same way this empirical standard is congenial to the incarnational thrust and pastoral instinct of the church. The church came into existence not to preserve a set of abstract teachings but to promote a way of life. Its ultimate norm is both practical and perceptible--love of God demonstrated by love of neighbor. This gives the church an inherent drive to be relevant to the real needs of real people and it checks transcendental, mystical, or escapist impulses. Of course, the tension between these two tendencies has not always been resolved smoothly in the history of the church, but an ecclesiology shaped by an empirical worldview certainly keeps the focus on what is primary in the constitution of the church.

At the same time, this empirical emphasis raises a twofold problem. On the one hand it suggests a pragmatic test of truth and relevance. This can lead to an overemphasis on numerical, financial, or attention-getting signs of success: how many converts, how many parishioners, how many clergy, how many attendees at a church event, how much money in the collection, how much coverage in the mass media, how big the Catholic vote. These quantifiable, observable indicators can take the place of the authentic, spiritual experience which should characterize the church.

On the other hand an empirical approach can diminish the importance of scholarship, reflection, and study, even fostering an anti-intellectual attitude in the name of pragmatic relevance. The church in the U.S. is especially susceptible to this shortcoming because of our culture's admiration for no-nonsense, can-do, get-results personalities. There is little patience with theorists, researchers, scholars, or deep thinkers in the public ethos, and virtually no one wants to be labeled impractical, out of touch, or living in an ivory tower.

The empiricism of process thought is not an invitation to be thoughtless or unreflective. On the contrary, its commitment to the primacy of facts is coupled with an equal commitment to interpret them. In doing so, process thought holds all intellectualizing, including the assertions of church dogma and policy, accountable to the real conditions of life and the disturbing features of reality which do not always fit cherished preconceptions. This openness to empirical verification also counteracts the tendency toward pastoral heresy.

Pastoral heresy is perpetuated by an idealistic (unreal) concept of the church imposed on the actual experience of church members. It privileges an abstract idea of the church as more real and important than the concrete reality of church life (an example of what Whitehead called the fallacy of misplaced concreteness). In contrast to this approach process ecclesiology values the complaints, dissatisfaction, and even rebellion of church members as a signal that the understanding, structuring, and enacting of church relationships may be deficient or erroneous.

In a process worldview the benefit of the doubt is always given to empirical experience. It is not the only word or the last word in church development but it is the most important word. In short, the empirical perspective of process ecclesiology fosters an ecclesial imagination that respects the stubborn facts of lived experience and draws from them inspiration and guidance for the ideals of church life.

An Aesthetic World

Whitehead viewed the world as a work in progress, each of its innumerable events responding in every instant to creative impulses from God and aiming at the fullest measure of satisfaction they can achieve. In this perspective the pervasive characteristic of the universe is creativity, and the ultimate aim of creative activity is a harmony of harmonies which coalesces into divine enjoyment. From start to finish Whitehead's vision is displayed as an aesthetic model of reality, fueled by feelings and a yearning for delight.

Such an aesthetic approach welcomes and values the role of novelty. New experience is the fruit of creativity and the antidote to boredom and repetition--the major threats to becoming in a creative, process worldview. But new experience is also unsettling; it disrupts established patterns and implicitly calls into question the adequacy of familiar and secure routines. The goal of an aesthetic worldview is to convert potentially disruptive novelties (such as a new form of church organization in small faith communities, new forms of theological assertion such as public dissent) into creative contrasts. A creative contrast is an innovation which is compatible with the overall character of an experience or activity (church community, critical theological reflection) while pushing the development of these forms and heightening the experience and meaning associated with them.

How does the aesthetic aspect of a process worldview contribute to ecclesial imagination? It stimulates the church to imagine itself as a work in progress, governed by aesthetic criteria and welcoming novel developments into its experience in contrast to the self-image of a completed organization committed to preserving its essential nature while allowing modified expressions of itself in order to communicate more effectively to a changing world.

The aesthetic emphasis of a process worldview harmonizes with an ecclesiology which affirms development and indulges in ritual celebration. The Catholic tradition does both. Change may come slowly and be severely tested before it is accepted, but Catholic ecclesiology has a place for both the development of doctrine and innovation in pastoral practice. In fact, this is one of the distinguishing traits of Catholicism. Historically it has led the Catholic church to develop doctrines and condone practices concerning Mary, the papacy, the sacraments, and life after death which other Christian groups judged to be excessive or erroneous additions.

The Catholic church also tends to ritualize everything and employ all the arts in expressing its beliefs. There is a long history of the church's patronage and preservation of the arts as well as the insertion of popular devotions and cultural expressions into Catholic experience, including the sacramental rites of the church. Although some of these practices play to sentimentality and reflect a superficial (and even superstitious) understanding of the faith, they bear witness to the church's aesthetic temperament and immersion in artistic expression.

The aesthetic aspect of a process worldview also poses a twofold problem for ecclesiology. First of all, it calls for aesthetic criteria rather than dogmatic or strictly logical criteria to evaluate new ideas and practices. Aesthetic criteria are less concerned with conforming to familiar, classic, or official standards than with promoting creativity and novelty. This does not mean that anything goes. In the aesthetic realm there are standards of excellence, beauty, and good taste which are used to form critical judgments about new works. And although there are experts and professional critics, aesthetic judgment is not confined to them. Ultimately it is a public task and the people as a whole decide what is and what is not aesthetically valuable in their culture. The goal of aesthetic judgment is to stimulate innovation and development, not to insure conformity to what is already known and established. In the final analysis the aesthetic question is not, "does this conform?" but, "does this work?"

Needless to say, aesthetic criteria are not the customary standards for evaluating new ideas and practices in the church. The primary criterion is continuity with tradition and the sources of faith rather than creativity and innovation which, more often than not, are treated with suspicion and skepticism. The act of judging is essentially an intellectual exercise, comparing new concepts (whether expressed in words or deeds) with normative teachings. Judgment is ultimately reserved to the episcopal magisterium rather than the church as a whole, and in the final analysis the hierarchical question is not, "does this work?" but, "is this true?"

Process ecclesiology recognizes this discrepancy and the tension it implies. Nonetheless it relies on the aesthetic judgment of the whole church (what Vatican II in the Constitution on the Church, no. 12, called the supernatural sense of the faith entrusted to the people of God by the anointing of the Spirit). This certainly includes and values both expert theological and official hierarchical assessments but it is not confined to them and in fact places them within the more inclusive, aesthetic judgment of the whole church.

The second problematic aspect of an aesthetic approach is that it can mask or minimize the reality of evil and sin which confronts human life, in the church as well as elsewhere. Process thought is often accused of falling into this trap because it tends to treat evil as a disruption of the intended or possible harmony in a given situation and to concentrate on the good or positive value which can be drawn from it. For the victims of evil this can seem like a weak, even repugnant, response typical of those who have never really suffered. For the perpetrators of evil it can seem like an invitation to rationalize the destructive effects of their evil acts by pretending that some good will result.

Sin, of course, is at the center of the story of salvation which the church proclaims. A soft interpretation of sin distorts the meaning and need of salvation and turns the church into another social club competing for members. Worst of all, it robs the cross of its prophetic and political power, converting it into little more than a piece of jewelry to make a fashion statement.

Process ecclesiology takes sin and evil very seriously but when confronted with their reality, it asks a different question from the classical worldviews on which traditional ecclesiologies are based.[5] Process thought does not assume that everything should follow a pre-established order in which good people should not be afflicted. It allows for the unpredictable, even chaotic, indeterminateness of creation and so when evil occurs, it does not ask, "why,?" but, "what now?" This seems to be preeminently God's question, judging from the accounts of Jesus' crucifixion. There was no answer to the anguished plea from the cross, "Why have you abandoned me?" But there was an answer to the hidden question (now what?) after Jesus' death—the resurrection. Process ecclesiology follows the same path in responding to the reality of sin and evil.

The aesthetic emphasis of process thought counteracts the tendency to pastoral heresy in two ways. By entrusting aesthetic judgment to the whole church, not just to experts or officials, process ecclesiology prevents responsibility for church relationships from being usurped by or relegated to a few. In the same vein if a significant number of the faithful indicate that a particular understanding, structuring, or enacting of church relationships is not working, it is a strong indication that something is wrong and needs to be corrected.

The second way process aesthetics counteracts pastoral heresy is by its preference for new developments. This preference prevents established patterns of interaction from escaping scrutiny and change. If new, contrasting experiences are not just welcomed but consistently promoted, it is less likely that practical wrongs which accompany an established way of doing things will be tolerated. The pastoral heresies associated with the European colonization of native American peoples and their religious traditions might have been avoided if an aesthetic criterion had guided the missionary practice of the time. The same is true even today with regard to the enduring assumption that a European expression of faith is superior to any other cultural expression of faith. In short, process ecclesiology imagines the church as a work in progress, to be judged by aesthetic standards which respond openly and creatively to novel contrasts.

A Panentheistic World

The dynamism of the organic world which appears empirically and is judged aesthetically is centered in the active presence of God. Whitehead made this very explicit in explaining his system, and theologians who have been attracted to his understanding of God have called it panentheism, meaning literally that all things are encompassed by God's experience. What God experiences is a complete grasp of the actual, empirical world in each moment of its becoming (the process equivalent of God's omniscience). This by itself would make God coextensive with the world (as in pantheism) but it would not make God more than the world (as implied in panentheism). For Whitehead God's experience includes more than what the whole world actually is. The "more" which God experiences is a feeling for the possibilities which the world might enact next, given its present state of becoming.

God's experience of the actual world is God's sense of its value in relation to these empirically-generated, ideal possibilities. This is what makes God more than the actual world and what enables the world to continue becoming. For God offers the divine experience back to the world as new aims which lure the world into its next moment of becoming.[6] This view of God is consistent with the dynamic nature of a process world and it affirms its organic, interactive quality as well. The world and God constantly, mutually interact and influence each other.

God's overall aim in this relationship is to stimulate the most creative, harmonious, and satisfying experience possible. In this respect the aesthetic model of process thought and the general aim of creativity predominate. God is actively involved in a work of co-creation with the world. God is not conceived as a finished entity one-sidedly creating, controlling, or culminating creation. God permeates the world, drawing from it and giving to it, feeling with it and beckoning beyond it, ceaselessly interacting and experiencing it.

How does the panentheistic aspect of a process worldview contribute to ecclesial imagination? It inclines the church to imagine itself as a process of co-creation with God which offers real, unforeseen contributions to God's experience rather than as a divinely-established community, fulfilling its mission in ways already known by God. This contrast is essentially the difference between a biblical and a philosophical understanding of God's relation to the world.

As noted above, it is striking enough that a modern philosopher like Whitehead would speak so candidly and emphatically of God's place in the scheme of things. It is even more appealing when the God he describes corresponds so well to the biblical portrayal of God who shares and creates history with the chosen people, offers them blessings, guides their development, challenges their pride, feels their rejection, cherishes their faithful, restores their dignity, and finally becomes one of them. The God of process thought corresponds quite well to this biblical experience, but not so well to the God of Christian philosophy whose attributes of perfection separate God from an incomplete, imperfect, in-process world.

On the other hand, the God of process thought poses two problems for ecclesiology. One is that Whitehead's God is unwaveringly monotheistic and the other is that his God is dangerously interdependent. Regarding the first point, Whitehead uniformly speaks of God in the singular (and even then in rather non-personal terms such as a principle of order, a source of novelty, a modifying agent, a locus of connection, the basis of relevance, the ideal harmony). While this raises questions about the adequacy of process thought for trinitarian theology, it also causes problems for ecclesiology. Ecclesiology is inseparable from christology, and the christology which the Catholic church professes is that Jesus is fully-human, fully-divine. If process theism is unable to affirm an adequate christology, any ecclesiology derived from it is also questionable.

A full response to this issue would go well beyond the scope of this book. Suffice it to say that Whitehead himself never addressed the nature of God as such. This was not his concern. He spoke of God insofar as his philosophical system called for the presence of a divine being. As a result, the capacity of process thought to articulate an adequate theology of the Trinity must be left to others. Among those who have taken up this challenge, Joseph Bracken stands at the forefront.[7] His work will be briefly reviewed in the next chapter, but for the present it may be said that he has given substantial reason to believe that process thought can consistently articulate a trinitarian theology.

On the other hand, it may legitimately be asked whether the actual belief of most Catholics is really trinitarian. Believers certainly affirm God as creator, speak of the Holy Spirit in their lives, and attribute divinity (or something like it) to Jesus. How their empirical belief corresponds to the dogmatic definitions of orthodoxy is another matter. Perhaps the creative, if tentative, speculations of process theology can actually strengthen a trinitarian awareness among the faithful.

In any event there is a second and experientially more significant problem with process theism. Although the interaction of God with the world, and especially with human beings, in a process of co-creation has many appealing features, it also confronts believers with a God who is not the all-powerful, all-knowing, all-directing deity they have imagined. Whereas the God of traditional belief freely chooses to be involved with creation, accepting the limitations and contingencies of a developing world but always capable of reverting to a more transcendent, powerful position in order to rescue the saints and insure salvation, the God of process thought is involved with creation and all its limitations by nature, as the chief exemplar of process reality, not an exception to it.

In this view God's traditional attributes are consistently redefined. God's omniscience means that God knows all there is to know, i.e., the actual events and experiences which comprise creation. What is not (the future) God does not know. Similarly, God's providence is not a long-range vision with accompanying plan which extends to the end of the world but an immediate vision of creation's next best possibilities as part of an ongoing process of becoming. God's power is not an intervening, controlling force making things turn out the way God wants but a persuasive appeal arising with the actual events of history beckoning creation to its most fulfilling experience. This image of God may not satisfy the customary desires and expectations of believers but it fits consistently a process worldview—and counteracts one rationale for pastoral heresy.

Pastoral heresy is predicated on a transcendent God whose relationship to the world, and the church, is the model for structuring human experience. Accordingly, church relationships are rightly defined, structured, and enacted by God's representatives who manage the spiritual well-being of everyone else. The thorough-going interdependence of God and creation in a process worldview replaces this model with a more collaborative form of interaction and removes the divine warrant for one-sided relationships of any kind. This does not eliminate the need for structure, the value of authority, or the role of leadership but it places all these elements in the context of a truly interdependent church. In short the panentheistic aspect of a process worldview imagines the church as a process of continual becoming embraced by God who is, as God, inherently and interminably involved in the co-creation of the church.

It should be clear from this overview that ecclesiology does not flow naturally and easily from a process worldview. The ecclesiology of process Catholicism does not come ready made; it must be constructed. So where in the dynamic, organic, empirical, aesthetic, panentheistic worldview of Alfred North Whitehead should one begin in order to construct a process ecclesiology? The answer to that question is in the next chapter.

Notes

1.   The major works of process ecclesiology are by Norman Pittenger, *The Christian Church as Social Process* (Philadelphia: Westminster Press) 1971; Bernard Lee, *The Becoming of the Church: A Process Theology of the Structure of Christian Experience* (Mahwah, NJ: Paulist Press) 1974; Marjorie Suchocki, *God-Christ-Church: A Practical Guide to Process Theology* (New York: Crossroad Publishing Co.) 1982. See also, John B. Cobb, Jr. and David Ray Griffin, "The Church in Creative Transformation" in *Process Theology: An Introductory Exposition* (Philadelphia: Westminster Press, 1976) 128-143; Joseph M. Hallman,

"Toward a Process Theology of the Church" in *Religious Experience and Process Theology: The Pastoral Implications of a Major Modern Movement*, eds. Harry James Cargas and Bernard Lee (Mahwah, NJ: Paulist Press, 1976) 137-147; Gordon E. Jackson, "Church: A Society of Caring" in *Pastoral Care and Process Theology* (Lanham, MD: University Press of America, 1981) 225-241.

2.   Among pastoral authors who use process thought, see Gordon Jackson, *Pastoral Care and Process Theology*, cited above; Bruce Epperly, *At the Edges of Life: A Holistic Vision of the Human Adventure* (St. Louis: Chalice Press) 1992; Larry Kent Graham, *Care of Persons, Care of Worlds* (Nashville: Abingdon Press) 1992; and Robert L. Kinast, *When a Person Dies* (New York: Crossroad Publishing Co.) 1984, *Sacramental Pastoral Care* (Collegeville, MN: The Liturgical Press, Pueblo Books) 1988, and *Let Ministry Teach* (Collegeville, MN: The Liturgical Press) 1996. In addition, the Process and Faith Program at the Center for Process Studies in Claremont, California offers publications, conferences, and other resources to bridge the gap between the technical, academic study of process thought and its pastoral usefulness.

3.   For helpful introductions to process thought and its implications for theology, see John B. Cobb, Jr. and David Ray Griffin, *Process Theology: An Introductory Exposition*, cited above and Robert Mesle, *Process Theology: A Basic Introduction* (St. Louis: Chalice Press) 1993.

4.   It should be noted that the best contemporary representatives of biblical theology, liturgical theology, and doctrinal theology also accent the dynamic, eventful quality of their disciplines. Process ecclesiology does not differ from these specialties in its appeal or emphasis but in its grounding—a philosophical understanding of reality rather than a scholarly understanding of the inherent nature of the Bible, the liturgy, and doctrine.

5.   Contrary to a widespread impression, process theologians have consistently and seriously wrestled with the problem of sin and evil. Among many examples, see Marjorie Hewitt Suchocki, *The Fall to Violence: Original Sin in Relational Theology* (New York: The Continuum Publishing Group) 1995; Bruce G. Epperly and Robert L. Kinast, *Can Suffering Be Redemptive?* (Claremont, CA: The Center for Process Studies) 1995; Jerry D. Korsmeyer, *Evolution and Eden: Balancing Original Sin and Contemporary Science* (Mahwah, NJ: Paulist Press) 1998.

6.   It is a debated point among process thinkers whether these aims are specific to each moment of each entity's becoming or more generic to types of entities and broad circumstances. For example, does the next aim in my becoming refer to the specific words I may choose to express the next thought in this sentence or does it refer to the broad activity of authoring a book on the topic of process ecclesiology or is it broader still, consisting in a general desire to write something for publication which may be helpful to others? This question has direct implications for understanding God's will or plan, and the corresponding responsibility to fulfill it.   My inclination is to

understand the aims for becoming in rather broad terms with maximum freedom for each individual to specify and concretize the realization of those aims. For an elaboration of this view, see David A. Pailin, *God and the Processes of Reality: Foundations for a Credible Theism* (London: Routledge) 1989.

7. Joseph Bracken is not alone in the development of trinitarian theology from a process perspective. See *Trinity in Process: A Relational Theology of God*, Joseph A. Bracken and Marjorie Hewitt Suchocki, eds. (New York: The Continuum Publishing Group) 1996.

Chapter 3

Elaborating a Process Worldview: Whiteheadian Societies

The general implications of Alfred North Whitehead's worldview for ecclesiology, sketched in the preceding chapter, can be made more specific by considering the work of Catholic theologians Bernard Lee and Joseph Bracken. Both have used Whitehead's philosophy of organism to develop their ecclesiology and trinitarian theology respectively.[1] I want to use their work to elaborate the key concept in Whitehead's system for constructing a process ecclesiology—his understanding of a society.

Bernard Lee's Process Ecclesiology

In his book, *The Becoming of the Church*, Bernard Lee uses process thought to explain the nature of the church and its sacramental life.[2] Four elements stand out in his presentation.

1. The key category in Lee's ecclesiology is Whitehead's notion of a <u>society</u>. For Whitehead, the term society refers to any composite entity, made up of individual elements, engaged in the process of becoming. Virtually everything we experience in our everyday world fits this description of a Whiteheadian society. Ordinary usage of the term, of course, is not so broad. Most people think of a society as an organized

group of living things, usually human beings, pursuing a common purpose. It takes a little effort to keep Whitehead's meaning in mind when using the term.

2. Lee affirms, with Whitehead, the critical role played by the <u>common form</u> of every society. It is the common form which holds the elements of a society together and gives them their identity as this event (a homily) rather than that event (a counseling session). For Lee, the common form of the church is the Jesus-event which he describes as bringing a new experience of the presence of God, an experience of God's all-embracing love. The importance of this event is that it provides a glimpse into the meaning of life as a whole.

3. The main concern of Lee's treatment, in terms of process reality, is the <u>reciprocity</u> between the individual components of a society and the society as a whole. He draws special attention to the twin objectives of every society—to combine its survival with the richest, most vibrant experience of becoming which it can achieve. Balancing these two elements is extremely difficult because they tend to go in opposite directions.

The most enduring things in the universe (metals, rocks, minerals) are those which exclude almost all change from their makeup. They are extremely unspecialized and appear to us to be inert. In this state most changes in the environment do not threaten their existence. The problem is that this type of stability militates against creativity and a richer experience of becoming. Rocks don't write poetry and minerals don't fall in love. On the other hand, more creative experiences of becoming, such as those in living cells, plants, animals, and humans, require specialized conditions which are harder to maintain and therefore make survival more difficult.

Applying this schema to the church, Lee contends that the solution to the survival problem is for the church to claim its unifying, common form in the least specialized way possible. Practically, this means insisting on the absolute minimum of specific doctrines while highlighting the church's generic features. In addition the church should treat its beliefs as ongoing, life-giving events rather than timeless truths or permanent substances (a distinction noted in the previous chapter). In this way the church's common form will enable it to endure in a variety of environments throughout time and in different settings rather than being dependent on specific circumstances which are hard to duplicate.

The solution to the second half of the dilemma, heightening the experience of becoming, is for the church to concretize its experience of itself in terms of the particular and changing conditions of its immediate environment (a perspective invoked regarding ecumenism in the previous chapter). To do this, the church asserts its common form as a dialectical partner with contemporary events. This rescues the church from isolation and increases the intensity of its experience through the resulting interactions. For Lee, this is the purpose of the church's sacramental life.

4. Church is best understood in a process framework as an <u>event</u> rather than an institution, and it is characterized by a high degree of pluralism rather than conformity. If its common form, the Jesus-event, is broadly understood so as not to overspecialize the kind of environment it needs to survive, then the church will also foster diversity and flexibility to intensify its experience of being church.

In his subsequent writings Lee has continued to use Whitehead's fundamental worldview to develop ecclesiological themes. In *Dangerous Memories*, co-authored with Michael Cowan, Lee examines the phenomenon of intentional communities and house churches as an alternative experience of church life.[3] In their treatment the authors explicitly refer to Whitehead in discussing the dynamics of human relationships and how they form a person's identity, the role of symbols and how they contribute to the formation of cultural images and worldviews, and the nature of the self or person as a dynamic, self-creative project.

In *The Future Church of 140 BCE* Lee exposes a hidden revolution taking place in the U.S. Catholic church.[4] It is a lay interpretation and enactment of church identity, parallel to the emergence of the lay Pharisaical movement in Judaism around 140 BCE. Pivotal to this development are three revolutions: the authority of experience, the transformation of power, and a rendezvous with history. Lee draws most fully upon Whitehead's views in explaining the first revolution--the nature and authority of experience, offering a brief "stroll through the megastory" which Whitehead told. He relies on the process theologian Bernard Loomer to discuss the transformation of power in the second revolution and adds Whitehead's voice to a host of others who have helped achieve a rendezvous with history by shifting emphasis from human persons as rational thinkers to human persons as rational agents.

What can one learn from Lee's treatment of the church that will help in constructing a process ecclesiology? First of all, the key category for understanding church is a Whiteheadian society. Second, the common form of the church should be defined broadly enough to support the church's survival but creatively enough to encourage its intensity (diversity) of experience. Third, the common form of the church derives from the event of Jesus, however that event is understood and kept alive. Fourth, the church is itself an event characterized by reciprocal interactions among its members and between them and the larger environments in which it functions. This has been the focus of Lee's attention in recent years. His reflections suggest that, fifth, process ecclesiology should highlight the actual relationships which currently constitute the church, especially those between small communities and larger church structures, between laity and clergy, and between the church as an identifiable society and the particular cultures in which it lives.

Joseph Bracken's Trinitarian Theology

Joseph Bracken's interest in Whiteheadian thought is both philosophical and theological, and in both areas he too concentrates on the Whiteheadian notion of society. Philosophically he sees the category of society as the foundational concept for a contemporary cosmology. Theologically he applies his understanding of society to the doctrine of the Trinity. His book, *Society and Spirit*, is the most complete presentation of his views, developing and synthesizing previously published works.[5]

For Bracken a society is an overlapping environment or field of activity which is conducive to the emergence of new occasions. On this point Bracken differs from Whitehead and other process thinkers by attributing a collective agency to the society as a whole. This collective agency is never independent of the activity of the individual members who constitute the society but neither is it relegated to one dominant member of the society as most interpreters of Whitehead, following Charles Hartshorne, maintain. The agency of a society is the cumulative experience of its member occasions (a point touched upon regarding the aesthetic judgment of the whole church in the previous chapter). This total experience conditions the becoming of new events in the life of that society. In Whiteheadian terms the common form of a society (for example, of a parish, a religious order, the Catholic church itself) is passed along to new members who take it into their becoming with slight, individual modifications. This explains the continuity from moment to moment which we experience in ourselves and most of the things around us.

The common form of a society is never fully realized in any particular occasion, but it is both intelligible and recognizable in the succession of events constituting the society. This may occur in one of two ways (already seen in Lee's treatment): either through a massive objectification of the common form with little variation or through the introduction of novel elements which maintain the common form while adapting to changes in the environment. In the latter case the novelties are localized at first, originating with certain occasions in the society and then gradually spreading throughout as others grasp the change and incorporate it into their becoming. Ecclesial examples of this process are the gradual spread of small faith communities since Vatican II and the hidden revolution of the laity's role in the church which Lee describes in *The Future Church of 140 BCE.*

Bracken applies these philosophical notions to an understanding of the Trinity and the relationship of a triune God to creation. Here again the central category is a society understood as a structured field of activity which interacts with other fields of activity. In the case of the Trinity, this means that "each of the divine persons is a subsistent field of (intentional) activity and that their ongoing interaction with one another results in a common field of intentional activity."[6]

In the trinitarian society the term Father designates the activity of proposing aims for new events in creation, the term Son designates the activity of responding to those aims, and the term Spirit designates the activity of mediating or harmonizing the two. This activity is completely creative, and because it encompasses all possibilities for becoming (the Father) as well as all actual occasions of becoming (the Son), it is equivalent to the organic whole of reality.

This whole may be understood as a cosmic society, consisting of interpenetrating fields of activity which occur within the encompassing field of God's trinitarian life. This is how Bracken understands the panentheism of process thought.

> [I]f the three divine persons of the Christian Trinity co-constitute by their interrelated activity an all-inclusive field within which the activities of all finite entities are located, and if the decisions of the divine persons from moment to moment impact upon their creatures and the self-constituting decisions of creatures are felt by the divine persons, then, one may legitimately say that God and creatures occupy a common world, a joint field of activity that all of them assist in shaping and forming.[7]

Bracken does not apply these insights to ecclesiology but certain implications stand out. First, the notion of society is central for understanding the realities of a process world, including the church. Second, a society (like church) may best be understood as a field of activity rather than a collection of individual entities (parishioners, theologians, Catholics) united by a single dominant factor (pastor, bishop, pope). This corresponds to Lee's urging that church be understood as event rather than institution or substance. Third, a society's field of activity is generated by the self-becoming of its members (the church is what it actually constitutes itself to be). This in turn objectifies the common element of form which allows new events to emerge and perpetuate the society. This is where the collective agency of a society is most operative. Fourth, every field of activity (every society) interacts with other fields in its general environment, eventually constituting the entire cosmic society; church is always influenced by and influences its larger environment.

Bernard Lee and Joseph Bracken have provided valuable guidance for constructing a process ecclesiology. In particular their emphasis on Whitehead's notion of a society warrants a closer look at this category and its implications for ecclesiology.

Whiteheadian Societies

Whitehead's most complete, and technical, treatment of societies is in his massive work, *Process and Reality*.[8] There, as in most of his philosophical writings, his primary intention was to explain the world of nature (cosmology). He rarely extended his analysis beyond the most basic elements that constitute the universe (cells, molecules, gases, etc.) although the implications of his analysis were always oriented toward a metaphysical worldview. Accordingly, Whitehead did not analyze the complex structure of a single human person very extensively, much less the extremely complex structures involving numerous human persons such as families, communities, governments, businesses, and, of course, church.[9] However, Whitehead did lay out the universal features which would characterize any society, including a mega-society like the church. These features and their implications for ecclesiology may be summarized as follows.

Multiplicity The first feature of a Whiteheadian society is its multiplicity. By definition, and in contrast to a single momentary occasion of experience, a society is a clustering (or nexus, as Whitehead frequently called it) of many occasions. In terms of ecclesial experience it is the coming together of discrete events such as worship, catechesis, mission, pastoral care coordinated into the single whole which is the church. In terms of ecclesial imagination this suggests that the church should be imagined, first of all, in its fullness, inclusive of the multiple events which constitute it. This calls for a thick description of church life rather than a reduction of it to an essential idea or an abstract principle.

Obviously it would be clumsy and counterproductive to mention all the main features of the church every time a person wants to use the word. Collective terms and abstract references are a practical necessity. However, the ecclesial imagination of process thought would be especially alert to two shortcomings in talking about the church in this way. The first is substituting a part for the whole. This occurs when people speak of "the church" but really mean the hierarchy or clergy (as in statements like "the church should stay out of politics" or "the church cares about its people"). It also occurs when Catholics are urged to pray for vocations, meaning an increase of candidates for the priesthood and religious life, not for all Christian vocations. Narrowing the full life of the church in this way feeds pastoral heresy because the particular individuals or groups who are equated with the church as such can easily assume that they should be the ones to determine how everybody else in the church should function.

The second shortcoming in talking about the church in general terms is a preoccupation with the church's essence or nature. An essentialist ecclesiology limits the fullness of church life to an irreducible core reality which distinguishes the church from everything else. In doing so, it tends to abandon the concrete events which constitute the actual experience of the church and substitute an idea (or ideal) of what the church is supposed to be (a prime example of misplaced concreteness). From the perspective of process ecclesiology, this is the seedbed of pastoral heresy because it imposes a concept of relationship, usually defined abstractly and one-sidedly, on the actual experience and conditions of the relationship.

The alternative to both of these shortcomings is an ecclesial imagination which draws inspiration from the actual life of the church and remains in contact with it as the source and norm of its description. An effective way to do this is to use images to describe the church, as Vatican II did in its major ecclesial documents (especially the Constitution on the Church, no. 6). As a symbolic expression, an image always carries a surplus of meaning, allowing for multiple interpretations of the multiple events which actually constitute the church and give rise to the image in the first place. Along with images, the ecclesial imagination of process thought values and relies on personal testimony, congregational case studies, scientific surveys, consultations, vignettes, anecdotes, and other data which remain close to the actual experience of church members. In all these ways process ecclesiology honors the fullness of church experience rather than substitute a part for the whole or dwell on the church's essence.

The emphasis on multiplicity in the makeup of a Whiteheadian society reflects the organic and empirical aspects of process reality. It takes into account everything that is actually part of a society's constitution. Accordingly, process ecclesiology should express the multiplicity (fullness) of the church in order to be consistent with the first feature of a Whiteheadian society.

Self-Constitution The second feature of a Whiteheadian society is the self-constituting character of its activity, reflective of the dynamic aspect of a process worldview. As self-constituting, a society comes into being through the activity of its members; it does not pre-exist that activity as a separate reality in its own realm of being. At the same time a society is a structured environment which fosters the kind of self-constituting activity which maintains and perpetuates the society as an identifiable reality.

Whitehead expressed this dynamic interaction between an environment and its events when he said, "A structured society as a whole provides a favorable environment for the subordinate societies which it harbors within itself."[10] Applied to ecclesiology this would mean that church is imagined as a favorable environment for the types of relationships among its members which are consistent with and constitutive of the meaning of church.

In Whitehead's account a society provides this favorable environment in one of two ways, which he called democratic or monarchical coordination. Although it is tempting to associate these terms with their modern political meanings, this was not how Whitehead used them. The gist of the distinction has already been seen in the explanations Bernard Lee and Joseph Bracken give for the two ways societies endure.

Democratic coordination means that all the member occasions share equally the experience of the society as a whole. This is best exemplified in the most basic elements of creation such as single cell organisms, gases, and rocks where one particle is virtually the same as every other. Moreover each member is completely dependent on the encompassing order of its societal environment and cannot survive apart from it. Democratic coordination minimizes novel events within its makeup and results in massive stability and endurance but at the expense of specialization, creativity, and intensity of experience.

Monarchical coordination means that one member (or cluster of members) in the environment of the society exercises a dominant influence over the others and organizes them to interact in such a way that the experience of the dominant member is enriched. This type of coordination is best exemplified in the animal/human world (which is as far as Whitehead took his analysis). It presupposes a highly complex center of activity such as a brain and nervous system for coordinating and communicating with the rest of the members (for example, the respiratory system, the circulatory system, the digestive system). Monarchical coordination relies on the incorporation of novel elements in the society's makeup and the integration of these novelties with the experiences of the other members resulting in creative adaptation and experience but at the risk of the society's stability and endurance.

There is a natural tendency to extrapolate from this description and imagine the multiple events of church life being coordinated either in a monarchical way (easily associated with a strong, centralized hierarchy as in Roman Catholicism) or in a democratic way (easily associated with a free-will, self-governing system as in a congregational tradition). Neither category as defined by Whitehead is adequate for the complex type of society which is the church. In the church each person is an individual, self-constituting center of activity (as Whitehead described) but also part of groups (a parish, a committee, a school, a religious order) which are relatively autonomous, coordinate their own activities, and make a distinct contribution to the church as a whole.

Given this complexity, perhaps the most accurate term for describing the coordination of the multiple events which constitute a mega-society like the church is organic. Not only is this Whitehead's preferred term for his worldview, but it also suggests varying layers of interaction between the parts and the whole of an environment. This sense of total interaction allows for variations and degrees of influence among the parts and between the parts and the whole, but always within the common environment. Consequently there is no single center of coordination (as in a monarchical society) nor is the common experience shared equally by all members throughout the whole environment (as in a democratic society). Rather the environment as a whole coordinates itself organically through the relationships shared by the multiple centers of activity which are its members in their various forms.

Applied to ecclesiology, one might say that church is a structured environment in which the activity of its members, especially their relationships to one another, is coordinated in an organic way. This means that they become who they are as members of the church through their various layers of interaction and thereby perpetuate the existence of the church as a whole. The relational activity of church members itself is relatively autonomous and creative, drawing partly on the already constituted experiences of the past and partly on the current experiences of living members.

The coordination of all this activity occurs organically through the shared sense of the church as a whole, made available at every moment in multiple forms such as symbols, representative persons, customs, language, and rituals. This awareness of the church's multiple centers of activity relating with various degrees of intensity, satisfaction, and completeness throughout the common environment coordinates the church's activity and counteracts the impulse toward pastoral heresy which arises when one center of activity seeks to control or dominate the others in the name of the church as a whole.

In the ecclesial imagination of process thought it is the sense of common environment, of organic relatedness rather than an overriding structure, authoritative office, or binding doctrine which coordinates the multiple, diverse experiences of church members and makes them one. It is also this sense of wholeness, renewed in every event of church life, which draws the church into continuous becoming and constitutes the third feature of a Whiteheadian society.

Propositional Appeal   Proposition is one of those familiar terms which Whitehead used in a distinct and unusual sense. It refers to a crucial moment in the ongoing process of becoming. As an event is nearing its completion, (e.g., the end of a liturgy or a pastoral visit), it generates a feeling for what it is about to become and what value it has for the next immediate occasion of experience. At this moment the future, which does not yet actually exist, enters into the makeup of the event as a real possibility.[11] As Whitehead expressed it, "The future is immanent in the present by reason of the fact that the present bears in its own essence the relationships which it will have to the future."[12]

In Whitehead's usage, a proposition is the desire for this immediate future, arising with the completion of the present. It is a pro-jection of what might be, given what is now becoming; it is a real (though not yet actualized) factor which re-presents the meaning of the experience just now being actualized as a lure for the next occasion in the series. This understanding of a proposition may seem to overlap with Whitehead's notion that God supplies the aims which initiate each new process of becoming. There is a close connection. A proposition is the impulse to continue the experience of becoming which is now coming to completion; it is wholly produced by and contained within the momentary experience itself. Divine aims combine this propositional impulse with the culmination of other, related events and the ideals which God envisions for creation as a whole. A proposition is, therefore, a constituent element in the formation of a divine aim but its origin and purpose are much more restricted.

Whitehead's analysis of propositional appeal was confined to the relatively simple societies of the natural world like molecules and plants. Applying it to a complex mega-society like the church, spread throughout the world and composed at any moment of billions of concrete events, is a staggering mental exercise. Nonetheless the same dynamics of propositional appeal which are at work in every other societal environment which makes up the world are also at work in the church.

The propositional appeal of a society originates with the activity of its members. The way they experience themselves in this moment (as a worshiping community, as a parish council, as a faculty of theologians) coalesces into a unified, definite feeling. This is the propositional quality of their activity within the society at that moment. It functions as a lure, enticing members with greater or lesser degrees of enthusiasm to continue experiencing themselves as part of this society—in the case of the church, as that part of the total ecclesial environment assembled in this space for Mass, in this parish for a meeting, in this school for teaching. Obviously if the preceding experience, and its antecedents, have been boring or oppressive, there will not be much incentive to perpetuate it. If this persists, the future of the church is threatened by the poor quality of its own experience. Of course, the opposite is equally true. In short, the continuation of any society, including the church, depends on the interest it generates from moment to moment.

This is the context for Whitehead's famous comment that "it is more important that a proposition be interesting than that it be true."[13] Insofar as truth reproduces the past, with its established order and settled experiences, it does not appeal much to creativity. Interest, on the other hand, channels attention toward the future, with its potential for new experiences and feelings of excitement. Ideally, of course, the most important propositions are those which are both true and interesting (similar to the ideal of a society to mate its survival with intensity of experience, as noted by Bernard Lee). Such a proposition summarizes a society's course of developments in such a way that it generates intense interest in actually experiencing the new possibilities it sets forth.

The meaning of propositional appeal for ecclesiology is best seen in the impact of the Second Vatican Council on the Catholic church. The council's ecclesial imagination, displayed most clearly in the final documents but permeating all of its proceedings, offered the members of the church an unexpected new way to experience themselves as Catholic.

The council's appeal drew upon an unwavering commitment to the church's origin and tradition along with a confident openness to modern developments. The result was an irresistible urge to become a renewed church rather than perpetuate the status quo which typically reinforces established patterns of relationship and can easily disguise pastoral heresies. The council's propositional appeal has continued to inspire and sustain church vitality to the present day (despite the tensions which have made the Common Ground Project a necessary undertaking)

From the example of Vatican II and from the general description of propositions in Whitehead's schema it should be clear that the propositional appeal to continuous becoming is an invitation to new experience, and this is the fourth feature of a Whiteheadian society.

Novelty Propositions arise from events as they are concluding but they appeal to the future and to the potential for new, satisfying experiences. This reflects the aesthetic dimension of a process worldview and is what lures a society into continuing its becoming. In a living society like the church, propositional appeal is increased to the degree that church members can anticipate novel experiences in the relationships which make them church. In the case of Vatican II this meant that the church could imagine itself as truly ecumenical and open to the spiritual truth of other religions, as celebrating a restored and communal liturgy with the full, conscious, and active participation of the worshipers, as supporting religious liberty for all people even if they choose not to act on it, as working cooperatively with others to solve contemporary problems, as expanding the roles of ministry for lay people in the church while prizing in a new way their secular vocation, as becoming again a biblical and evangelizing people.

The most stimulating kind of new experience for a society like church is one that contrasts with previous experience (for example, Vatican II's reversal of ecumenical policy or its decision to celebrate the liturgy in the vernacular). Novel contrasts intensify the feelings associated with belonging to a given society and heighten the value of the interactions within it. This is a further reflection of the aesthetic character of process reality which Whitehead summarized as follows: "all aesthetic experience is feeling arising out of the realization of contrast under identity."[14] Just as the enjoyment of music or dance or art is increased (intensified) when contrasting sounds or movements or shapes are introduced, so the feeling of belonging to the church is increased when contrasting experiences are introduced into the ecclesial environment.

Intensifying the experience of belonging to the church through novel contrasts is not a matter of numerical or quantitative increase; it concerns the quality of experience shared by people interrelating with one another. It is precisely a desire for this kind of experience which has stimulated the formation of small faith communities since Vatican II. Intensity of experience is the goal, and novelty is the catalyst. In this respect experimentation and innovation are essential to the life of a society like church.

Moreover, the cultivation of novel experiences enhances the church's survival. Novelty is an incitement to continue experiencing the heritage of the church's past but in even more stimulating and fulfilling ways. This generates enthusiasm for the future and increases the flexibility (as well as the desire) of church members to incorporate novel elements (such as women's equality, lay ministry, inculturation) into their experience of church, enabling them to adapt more effectively to unexpected or undesired changes in their environment. This is an ecclesial example of the general position Whitehead articulated: "By reason of this flexibility of structural pattern, the society can adopt that special pattern adapted to the circumstances of the moment."[15]

The value, as well as the survival, of a living society like the church depends on the novel contrasts it includes in its experience of becoming. Preservation alone does not guarantee value or prevent pastoral heresy. In fact, without novel contrasts the propositional appeal of the church will decline and be replaced by an abstract principle of repetition and conformity which encourages pastoral heresy. With novel contrasts the propositional appeal of the church remains vigorous and makes pastoral heresy less likely. However, this will happen only if the novel contrasts incorporated into the church's life are compatible with its common form, which is the fifth and most important feature of a Whiteheadian society.

Common Form   The common form is best understood as a pattern or structure of experience, permeating the environment of a society and giving the activity of its constituent members a common identity as belonging to this society (the church) rather than a different society (a nation, business, school). In doing so, the common form also perpetuates the society by sustaining the pattern of relationship among the members of the society from one experience to the next.

Sustaining a society's pattern of relationship (and its continuation in existence) does not mean imposing it intact on succeeding occasions. It means proposing it for new occasions to make it part of their experience and thereby to perpetuate the society. In this respect the common form is similar to a proposition, described above.   The difference is that a proposition pertains only to a moment of experience, beckoning its continuation in the next immediate moment, whereas the common form pertains to the pattern of experience which defines or characterizes the society as a whole, inclusive of all its experiences.   For this reason Whitehead also referred to the common form as the defining characteristic of a society.

The common form is not just a class name or mental category arbitrarily applied to diverse elements, uniting them nominally or conceptually.[16] The common form has a "genetic" relationship to the members of the society because it comes into being through the events and experiences of the members themselves and the members make it part of their ongoing experience as the society. Whitehead expressed this reciprocal dynamic as follows.

> The reproduction of the common form throughout the nexus [environment of the society] is due to the genetic relations of the members of the nexus among each other, and to the additional fact that genetic relations include feelings of the common form. Thus the defining characteristic [common form] is inherited throughout the nexus [society], each member deriving it from those other members of the nexus which are antecedent to its own concrescence [experience of becoming].[17]

But how does the common form of a society come to be in the first place? It comes to be through the interrelationships of the members who constitute the society; it arises with their experience of one another. The common form of a society does not pre-exist the events which constitute the society; it does not endure in and of itself like a laboratory where experiments occur or an empty church building where liturgy is celebrated. The common form of a society is always and only part of the actual becoming of that society.

Once events begin to cluster and experience one another in a certain way, they form a pattern, and this pattern exerts varying degrees of influence on future events moving them to experience themselves more or less in harmony with the pattern that has been established. This is the collective agency of a society which Joseph Bracken speaks about. It pivots around the common form which holds all of the society's activity together, giving it a shared identity and continuity.

Because the common form arises within the life of the society and as part of its continual self-creation, it is neither immutable nor inevitable. It is constantly being modified by new experiences while retaining a sufficient, recognizable identity. The most familiar example of this is the development of a single human being from infancy through old age. In a living society like the church with multiple centers of relatively autonomous activity the common form will exhibit a high degree of flexibility and dynamism. Its continuity and commonality may not be so obvious when events from its origin (New Testament communities) are juxtaposed with much later events (medieval Christendom or twentieth century ecumenism). That is why the common form of an enduring society must be seen in the entire course of its becoming in order to recognize how it maintains the identity of the society.

The common form does not guarantee that new events will experience themselves in harmony with the pattern already established, even allowing for degrees of flexibility and adaptation in that pattern. It is always possible that new events will structure themselves in ways that are incompatible with existing patterns of experience. In human history this happened, for example, when slavery was rejected as the common form of economic and social life, when monarchy was rejected as the common form of political life, when submission to the bishop of Rome was rejected as the common form of Christian life. Changes of this magnitude do not happen all at once but they do happen, radically undercutting the assumption that existing patterns of relating must inevitably endure (a presupposition of pastoral heresy).

Applying this principle to the church means that church members in their concrete interactions (relationships) ultimately determine what church actually is. There is no extra-ecclesial divine authority which intervenes to set the church apart as an exception to the dynamics of a Whiteheadian society. The church's divine authority is inherent in, intrinsic to the dynamics of church life. It is expressed in the common form of church and made manifest in the twofold interaction (relationship) of church members among themselves and the church with the other societies which make up the world.

In less technical terminology, one might say that the church is a structured environment in which people relate to one another through a common identity and thereby become who they are as members of the church while perpetuating the existence of the church itself. The common identity arises in part from the already constituted church and in part from the living members who currently constitute and prolong it into the future.

The church as already constituted contributes what has been experienced up to this point, its history as a church expressed in multiple forms with different degrees of importance and appeal (e.g., Scripture, sacraments, doctrine, pastoral praxis). Living members contribute their creative appropriations of this heritage. The entire interaction is coordinated by the common form which expresses the essential identity of the church and integrates novel appropriations into its cumulative past.

The key element in this whole process which distinguishes one society from another is its common form or defining characteristic. As already noted, the common form of the church is centered in Jesus. Without him, there is no church. Consequently, the task of constructing a process ecclesiology and exercising ecclesial imagination from a process perspective must take account of Jesus as the common form of the church. This is the topic of the next chapter.

Notes

1.   It should be mentioned that another Catholic theologian, Donald Gelpi, has offered sympathetic but incisive criticisms of Whitehead's system which, in his view, make it unsuitable for theological use. See Donald L. Gelpi, *The Turn to Experience in Contemporary Theology* (Mahwah, NJ: Paulist Press, 1994) 52-90. A full response to Gelpi's critique would go beyond the purpose of this section but the following comments are appropriate. Gelpi raises two basic criticisms: there is no real generality in Whitehead's system but only self-contained individual events, and there is no coherent explanation of continuity from moment to moment and event to event. I believe that Whitehead's principle of creativity which characterizes each event of becoming does establish real generality throughout the organic continuum and his notion of propositional appeal arising at the conclusion of each event and eliciting new events explains continuity. These points will be elaborated in the course of this chapter.

2.   See Bernard J. Lee, *The Becoming of the Church*, cited in chapter two, note one.

3.   See Bernard J. Lee and Michael A. Cowan, *Dangerous Memories: House Churches and Our American Story* (Kansas City, MO: Sheed and Ward) 1986.

4.   See Bernard J. Lee, *The Future Church of 140 BCE: A Hidden Revolution* (New York: Crossroad Publishing Co.) 1995.

5.   See Joseph A. Bracken, *Society and Spirit: A Trinitarian Cosmology* (Selinsgrove, PA: Susquehanna University Press) 1991. See also *The Triune Symbol: Persons, Process, and Community* (Lanham, MD: University Press of America) 1985 and *The Divine Matrix* (Maryknoll, NY: Orbis Books) 1996.

6.   See Joseph A. Bracken, *Society and Spirit*, 129.

7.   Ibid., 140.
8.   See Alfred North Whitehead, *Process and Reality*, corrected edition by David Ray Griffin and Donald W. Sherburne (New York: The Free Press, 1978) 83-110.
9.   This is another reason why Donald Gelpi does not think Whitehead's system is useful for theological reflection. It is a major leap from analyzing the complex activity of a cell or molecule to the interactions of nations or churches. He rightly cautions process thinkers against taking Whitehead's terminology and using it as if it fits worship, mission, or pastoral care without adaptation. I hope to show that Whitehead's understanding of a society is applicable to the church by adhering to his basic understanding while elaborating it as necessary.
10.   See Whitehead, *Process and Reality*, 99.
11.   Whitehead's understanding of a proposition responds to Donald Gelpi's criticism that process thought is trapped in a bi-polar model of reality and can explain neither the transition from one self-contained event to another nor the continuities we observe in the everyday world of experience. Gelpi prefers the tri-polar model of Charles Peirce. I believe that Whitehead's propositions are the equivalent of Peirce's third element and provide the explanation which Gelpi finds lacking.
12.   See Alfred North Whitehead, *Adventures of Ideas*, 194.
13.   Ibid., 244.
14.   See Alfred North Whitehead, *Process and Reality*, 280.
15.   Ibid., 100.
16.   This is another of Donald Gelpi's criticisms of Whitehead's system, that it is guilty of conceptual nominalism because there is no real continuity between events. However, if propositions establish real connections between momentary events and if the common form of a society produces genetic relations among its members, then Whitehead's explanation is no more an example of conceptual nominalism than is the explanation of Peirce, whom Gelpi favors.
17.   See   Alfred   North   Whitehead,   *Process   and   Reality*,   34.

Chapter 4

The Origin of the Church:
Jesus' Relationships

Jesus of Nazareth did not found a church. He formed relationships which challenged and changed the people around him. From that core experience there emerged a new way for people to relate to one another. The appeal of this new way of living together gradually gave shape to what we now call the church of Jesus Christ. At the heart of this development, holding it together and giving it continuity through the ages, are the relationships of Jesus. In terms of a process worldview they are the common form of the society known as the church. As such, the relationships of Jesus require a closer examination as the key element in constructing a process ecclesiology.

The primary and most reliable guide for understanding Jesus' relationships are the canonical gospels. The gospels, of course, are not documentaries or detailed accounts of everything Jesus said and did. They are proclamations of faith, asserting who Jesus was and what his life meant to those who believed in him. It is from this perspective that the stories of his encounters and relationships with others must be read, and it is this same perspective which should guide the application of the biblical witness to process ecclesiology.

Following the empirical emphasis of process thought and its experience-to-theory approach, I will first examine Jesus' actual relationships, then reflect on the nature and importance of relationships for Jesus, and conclude with a description of how his relationality should function as the common form of the church today.

JESUS' RELATIONSHIPS

In general, the gospels depict all of Jesus' relationships as shaped by and subsumed into his relationship with God. This relationship was so novel and all-inclusive for Jesus that he gave it his own unique designation--the reign of God.[1] How was this expressed in Jesus' actual relationships with people?

Jesus and His Disciples

Although Jesus is frequently referred to as a rabbi and his disciples are mentioned throughout the four gospels, his interaction with them does not fit the standard model of a rabbi and disciples. Unlike conventional rabbis Jesus did not have a fixed set of scholarly biblical interpretations which his disciples had to master nor did he seek the deference and formal respect accorded to rabbis. His instruction dealt more with how to live than how to interpret texts; he did not require exact repetition of his teachings (at least if the variations in the four gospels are any indication); and he substituted service of others for professional prestige and honor.

And yet, Jesus accepted the title, rabbi, and seemed to be always surrounded by disciples. Exactly who these disciples were is not easy to determine.   There are at least three groups mentioned in the gospels. First, there are the crowds of disciples in Luke's gospel, to whom the beatitudes are addressed (LK 6:17) and who accompany Jesus into Jerusalem (LK 19:37). There are also "the many disciples" in John 6:60 who find Jesus' teaching on the bread of life too difficult to accept.

Second, some disciples from these crowds apparently wanted to follow Jesus more closely or more often (MT 8:18-22; LK 14:25). Jesus makes it clear to them what will be involved (MT 10:37-38; LK 9:57-62). Perhaps the story of the rich young man (MT 19:16-22) fits this category.   Among those who regularly accompanied Jesus, although they are not called disciples, are the women who offered provisions out of their own resources (LK 8:1-3). Luke also describes the mission of the seventy (or seventy two) disciples whom Jesus sent in pairs ahead of him to the villages he wanted to visit (LK 10:1-12). And in addition to these specific groups there are numerous references to "the disciples" who hear Jesus' teachings and observe his deeds.

Third, the most distinct group of disciples are the Twelve whom Jesus himself selected (MK 3:13-19). Initially they shared in Jesus' mission of proclaiming the reign of God with the accompanying signs of exorcism and healing--not the typical functions of a rabbi's disciple. This missionary role is reiterated after Jesus' resurrection (MT 28:16-20) although in Luke's version (LK 24:44-45) other disciples are with the eleven at the time of the great commission.

The Twelve sometimes received more detailed explanations than the rest of the disciples about the meaning of Jesus' parables and actions but they are invariably portrayed as neither understanding his teaching nor possessing the faith to act on it. This unflattering portrait accents the novelty of Jesus' relationship with them, for their primary role was not to propagate his rabbinical opinions or eventually take their place in the rabbinic tradition following their tutelage but to bear witness to him.

Perhaps the most revealing aspect of the Twelve is their number. This is ordinarily associated with the original twelve tribes of Israel and is assumed to symbolize the beginning of a new Israel, although Jesus does not confirm this explicitly. When he responds to Peter's question about the reward they will receive for following him, Jesus depicts them sitting on twelve thrones judging the twelve tribes of Israel (MT 19:28; LK 22:30). This symbolic role seems unique to the original Twelve because after Judas is replaced (Acts 1:15-26), there is no further indication of preserving a structure of just twelve disciples, whereas their missionary and witnessing role is continued and expanded (especially by Paul).

From a process perspective two things are striking about Jesus' relationship with his disciples. First of all, it is novel in comparison with the standard rabbi-disciple relationship of the time, a novelty which required an adjustment in the customary pattern of relating (the common form) between rabbis and their disciples. When such adjustments are called for and refused, pastoral heresy usually ensues. Second, it is an inclusive relationship with degrees of difference. There were varying levels of discipleship based on a more or less complete conformity to the life Jesus lived, and yet the various levels were all unified by their common association with him—an example of the organic coordination described in chapter three and an antidote to pastoral heresies resulting from dualistic or separatist ways of thinking.

Jesus and Women

The most fundamental human relationship is that between men and women. Citing men first in this relationship is not accidental. This has been the pattern in most societies, and it was no different at the time of Jesus. In fact the dominance of men was more pronounced and the recourse of women was more limited than in our day. How did Jesus relate to women?

From the incidents recorded in the gospels Jesus seems to have related to women in an open, mutual, respectful manner that deviated from the established pattern of his time.[2] He was certainly aware of the social and religious customs and expectations of his culture, but he did not seem to feel bound by them. Neither was he a feminist in the modern sense of the term; he did not set out to champion the dignity and rights of women. What was the basis for his novel treatment of women?

As mentioned at the outset of this section, Jesus was fixated on the reign of God. He interpreted everything in terms of this all-encompassing relationship. When he met women, he invited them to experience God's reign just as he invited men to do. The classic instance of this is his discussion with the woman at the well in John 4:1-42. When he saw women manifesting attitudes and performing actions consistent with God's reign, he drew attention to them, holding them up as models for others. Examples are the woman with hemorrhages whose faith led to her healing (MK 5:25-34), the poor widow who contributed to the temple treasury out of her scarcity (MK 12:41-44), and the sinful woman who anointed Jesus at the home of Simon, the Pharisee (LK 7:36-50). With regard to healing, Jesus was more proactive with women than with men, perhaps reflecting a societal restriction preventing women from taking initiative and asking for help. Examples of this are his raising to life the son of the widow of Nain (LK 7:11-15) and the healing of a woman crippled for eighteen years (LK 13:10-13).

Jesus' free, open way of relating with women raises two important questions from a process perspective: how did women affect Jesus and why did he not include women among his hand-picked Twelve? The first question is important in light of the process emphasis on interrelatedness and mutual influence in relationships. The second is important in light of the process orientation toward inclusiveness.[3] The answer to both questions is necessarily speculative, because they are not biblical concerns. However, the gospels do provide a few glimpses which are worth examining

Perhaps the clearest example of the way certain women seemed to affect Jesus was the Canaanite woman who asked him to heal her daughter (MK 7:24-30). When Jesus finally responded, he told her in colloquial language that his mission was only to the Jews. The woman answered in kind, applying the metaphor of feeding dogs to her situation, thereby manifesting the faith Jesus sought in Israel and changing his decision to help her child. A second example, which appears to be a dramatic reconstruction, is the Samaritan woman at the well. She seemed to intrigue Jesus and elicit from him a sharing of faith that more than satisfied the physical hunger and thirst he had initially felt (JN 4:34-38). And of course there is Mary, the sister of Martha and Lazarus, who moved Jesus to tears when she asked why he had not come sooner to help the dying Lazarus and then moved him to action when she led him to the tomb of her dead brother (JN 11:28-44).

What of his own mother? How did Jesus relate to her? The evidence is sketchy. Apart from the infancy narratives, which have dubious historical reliability, and the assumption that Mary was influential in his upbringing, there are few occasions when Mary appears in the gospels. If the wedding feast at Cana (JN 2:1-11) is a factual account, it indicates that she altered his initial reaction to her request (similar to the Canaanite woman's influence). At the end of John's gospel (JN 19:26-27) Jesus is portrayed as looking after Mary's welfare by entrusting her to the beloved disciple.

The most telling event is the time when Mary and her family came to see Jesus (MK 3:31-35) after other relatives had tried to seize him (MK 3:21). His reaction sounds like a rejection of them but it can be properly interpreted as Jesus using the occasion to dramatize his understanding of the reign of God. In place of the unequal relationships which prevailed in the family structure of his time, all who heard (i.e., embraced) the Word of God were equally members of Jesus' family. If this was true, why didn't Jesus include women in his selection of the Twelve?

The question is difficult to answer because, as noted above, Jesus did not give a clear rationale for selecting the Twelve. If the standard explanation is correct that he wanted to symbolize the beginning of a new Israel, then it would have made sense for him to select twelve men since families took their identity from the father/husband. This would not have contradicted his view of women so much as conceded to the limitations of his situation and the desire to have his symbolic action understood.

On the other hand, the Twelve do not seem to play an indispensable or unique role in the ministry of Jesus. The seventy [two] were given the same mission and virtually the same power. As noted above, the Twelve showed no special adeptness at understanding Jesus' teachings or interpreting his actions, and after his resurrection they did not endure as a permanent structure, at least not as the Twelve. In contrast, the women who accompanied Jesus remained with him during his passion while the Twelve and all other disciples abandoned him, and they were the first messengers of his new life. In light of this, the exclusion of women from the Twelve seems less significant than their inclusion, and leadership, in spreading his word after the resurrection.

From a process perspective Jesus' relationship with women is striking in two ways. First, his freedom and openness in relating to women was a novel contrast in the established pattern of male dominance at his time, a pattern which would constitute a pastoral heresy wherever it is found today. Jesus apparently was not controlled by pressure from the past when responding to new experiences in the present. Second, Jesus' relationship with women was not an end in itself; it was governed by his overriding relationship with God. This relationship, symbolized as the reign of God, was the unifying principle for everything in his life and the source for overcoming pastoral heresy. It took precedence over custom and learned behavior in human relationships. By the same token it allowed him to affirm women as models for others when they manifested the meaning of the reign of God.

Jesus and the Priests

It is sometimes said that Jesus was a lay man rather than a priest. Given his family of origin, Jesus had no choice. Priesthood was not a voluntary profession as it is today; it was the privilege of certain tribes and the families within those tribes. This arrangement set priests apart from the rest of the people, especially in their role as custodians of the cult and protectors of the spiritual knowledge of God. In these capacities they were regulators of the ritual and overseers of moral cleanliness. How did Jesus relate to the priestly class of his day?

Jesus' relationship with the priests, like his relationship with women, was determined by his vision of God's reign. Whenever he saw distortions of the proper relationship with God, especially when ritual requirements took precedence over human need, he opposed it. For example, when challenged by the priests to justify his disciples' eating grain on the Sabbath to abate their hunger, he referred to the much more outrageous act of David and his men eating the bread set aside for the priests (MK 2:23-68). In the parable of the good Samaritan he implicitly chastised the priest (and the Levite) for preserving their ritual purity and passing by the man who had been mugged rather than stopping to help as the Samaritan did (LK 10:31).

Despite his critiques, Jesus did not oppose the priestly office as such. On two occasions when he cured lepers (MK 1:44, LK 17:14), he told them to show themselves to the priests so they could be certified as clean and rejoin their communities. What Jesus opposed was the loss of the cult's meaning over which the priests presided. When Jesus urged people to adopt a childlike freedom and spirit in their relationship with God, this was not intended to abolish sacrifice and temple worship but to restore the attitude which should imbue both.

When Jesus arrived in Jerusalem, he took two actions which antagonized the chief priests. The first was the cleansing of the temple (MK 11:15-18). This was a multi-layered symbolic action. Simultaneously it recalled the purpose of the Temple to be a house of prayer; it exposed the corruption of that purpose by the toleration of inappropriate practices; and it established Jesus as the one with authority to safeguard God's house.

The second action Jesus took was to teach in the temple area (JN 7:14-31, LK 22:52-53). His teaching was not uncontested. The chief priests (along with other officials) wanted to know by what authority he did this. Jesus countered their question with a query of his own about the authority of John's baptism (MT 21:24-27) and followed it up with the parable of the tenants (MT 21:33-45) which the priests correctly understood as intended for them. Jesus' response stymied their inquiries but solidified their opposition. From that point on, the chief priests became the prime architects of the plot to kill him (LK 19:47).

It was they who brought the initial religious charge against him and colluded with the Roman authorities to carry out the execution. Even then they objected to the way Pilate proclaimed Jesus' crime (JN 19:21) and they prevailed upon him to post a guard at the tomb to insure that his disciples would not dupe the people into believing he had risen from the dead (MT 27:62-64).

All in all, the gospels give the impression that Jesus' relationship with the chief priests was antagonistic, conflictual, and ultimately fatal. They seemed unable to find a common ground on which they could relate. Jesus criticized the way they performed their duties and held them publicly accountable, claiming as his authority the very honor of God.

From a process perspective this relationship exemplifies the priority of practice over formality and indicates how difficult it can be to balance intensity of experience with structures of survival (one of the basic issues in Whitehead's understanding of a society, as elaborated by Bernard Lee).

In a process worldview practice, or the actual experience of becoming, always takes precedence over formal or nominal claims to importance. This is consistent with the dynamic and empirical emphases of process reality and is the chief counterforce to pastoral heresy. At the same time all creative activity, which is the ultimate aim of becoming, requires a suitable order or structure. Ideally the interplay between the two is an aesthetic adventure but factually, both in the natural world and in human relationships, it is often a bitter and exhausting struggle which can end in failure. Despite its overall optimism and aesthetic appreciation, process thought is not naive about what it takes to achieve the creative harmony God desires.

Jesus and Religious Leaders

At the time of Jesus the most prominent groups of religious leaders were the scribes, the Pharisees, and the Sadducees. The scribes were the scholars of tradition, the literate class who mastered the history of interpretation and preserved the accumulated meaning of texts and commentaries. They were highly respected authorities for their knowledge of tradition. Most scribes were probably also Pharisees, spiritual zealots who conceived Israel as a religious nation grounded in a strict interpretation of the Mosaic Law. Their theocratic orientation made them somewhat apolitical, at least in contrast to the Sadducees who had once ruled Judea under the Hasmoneans (163-35 BCE) and were always looking for the best accommodation to Roman control they could find.

Jesus should have appreciated the Pharisees' devotion to fulfilling the Law and their priority on the religious character of Israel vis-à-vis the political maneuverings of the Sadducees with the Romans. Likewise he should have appreciated the scholarship of the scribes and the lively repartee they invited because of their erudition and mastery of various schools of interpretation. And yet the gospels indicate that his relationship with all these groups was no better than his relationship with the priests, despite the fact that some Pharisees warned him of Herod's desire to kill him (LK 13:31) and several Pharisees invited Jesus to their homes for dinner. As reported by Luke, the conversation during these meals turned to controversy with Jesus denouncing the attitudes and practices of the Pharisees (LK 7:36-50; 11:37-54; 14:1-14). Indeed some of Jesus' most caustic and judgmental pronouncements were aimed at the scribes and the Pharisees (MT 23).

The Pharisees, especially, manifested two qualities which Jesus could not abide. Their rigor and strictness in interpreting the Law blinded them to its spirit and purpose and most of all to the God who gave it. Similarly, their dedication and learning fostered an elitist self image which caused them to look down on the rest of people (JN 7:49), create obstacles in their relationship with God (MT 23:4), and overlook their own hypocrisy. These attitudes contradicted the meaning of God's reign as Jesus understood it. Whereas he came to call the "sick," the moral, religious, and social outcasts, into the reign of God, the scribes and Pharisees scoffed at his association with them (MK 2:13-17). Jesus turned their arrogance against them when he extolled the prayer of a tax collector over that of a Pharisee (LK 18:9-14).

The Sadducees did not fare much better, especially when they joined with their natural antagonists, the Pharisees, against Jesus. Like John the Baptist who questioned the sincerity of their repentance (MT 3:7-9), Jesus doubted their ability to read the signs of the times (MT 16:1-3) and easily overcame their clumsy attempt to trap him in a question about the resurrection of the dead (MT 22:23-33).

The scribes may have found a little more favor with Jesus. At least one of them wanted to follow him (MT 8:19) and another proved himself not far from the reign of God by agreeing with Jesus' answer regarding the greatest commandment (MK 12:34). Some scribes

approved his response to the Sadducees about the resurrection of the
dead (LK 20:39) and Jesus speaks of scribes who have been instructed
in the kingdom of heaven (MT 13:52), perhaps indicating that some of
them were among his disciples.

Nonetheless the overall impression is that Jesus did not enjoy a very
good relationship with the religious leaders of his time. He respected
their office and even told the people to follow their teachings (MT
23:3) but he rejected their personal practice and the attitude of self-
importance that accompanied it. For Jesus elitism and hypocrisy
contradict the reign of God.

From a process perspective this relationship shows that the
introduction of novel elements into an established order requires an
adjustment of the common form of that order. When Jesus began to
include tax collectors, prostitutes, and other sinners in his company, it
required a new interpretation of the Law and its tradition (even if it
was an old interpretation, renewed). In part the image of the reign of
God signaled this change. It was not intended to replace the Law but
to reconfigure it so its meaning could be experienced authentically and
creatively. The scribes, Pharisees, and Sadducees adhered too rigidly
and one-sidedly to their inherited interpretations (the epitome of
pastoral heresy) to entertain such a development. As a result, they
placed themselves outside the scope of Jesus' inclusive reign.

Jesus and Minorities

The Romans, though numerically small in Israel, exercised the
controlling force of a majority power. This put all Jews in a
subordinate position and exacerbated the already tense relationships
between Jews and other groups in the region. With no one were these
relations more strained than with the Samaritans.

The Samaritans were a mixed breed of Jews who were looked upon
as schismatics, if not heretics, in their worship and religious practices.
The most contentious point between Jews and Samaritans was temple
worship, dating back to the restoration of the temple in Jerusalem
under Zerubbabel (537-515 BCE). The alienation intensified when the
Samaritans sided with the Seleucids during the Maccabean wars (165-
161 BCE). The relationship between Jews and Samaritans was so bad
that a clear sign of contempt was for one Jew to call another a
Samaritan--as some of the Jews referred to Jesus (JN 8:48).

In contrast to this hostile and bitter attitude Jesus displayed
remarkable acceptance of Samaritans. When a Samaritan village

would not welcome him because he was on his way to Jerusalem, Jesus rebuked the instinctive reaction of James and John who wanted to call down fire from heaven to consume them (LK 9:51-56). More than this, Jesus used a Samaritan to dramatize what it means to be a neighbor (LK 10:29-37) and he praised the faith of the Samaritan leper who alone returned to give thanks after being healed (LK 17:16). Perhaps Jesus' attitude toward Samaritans is best displayed in his meeting with the Samaritan woman at the well, already mentioned.

It is true that Jesus instructed the Twelve not to go to Samaritan towns on their missionary travels (MT 10:5), but this is a reflection of his initial focus on Israel, not a rejection of Samaritans or a perpetuation of Jewish antipathy toward them. On the contrary Jesus manifested the same attitude towards the Samaritans as he did toward women, and for the same reason. If they exemplified the meaning of God's reign and if they showed a corresponding faith, Jesus acknowledged this and praised them without reservation or qualification.

From a process perspective the relationship of Jesus with Samaritans (as with women and other disparaged groups) suggests that he may have deliberately sought out experiences which would be startling and confronting to established expectations. In this respect he was proactive rather than reactive; in process terms he had a preference not just for novelty but for novel contrasts. Novel contrasts increase the quality of experience and promote greater creativity than do mere repetition and reenactment, which incline toward pastoral heresy. The former is what God seeks, and Jesus, given his intimate relationship with God, seems to have sought out, and possibly even provoked, novel contrasts to satisfy this divine aim.

Jesus and non Jews

Jesus' attitude toward Samaritans extended to the Gentiles, and in much the same emotional context. Jews referred to Gentiles in derisive, unflattering terms as being inferior to themselves morally and spiritually. Jesus reflected this common mentality when he contrasted his expectations regarding love of enemies, prayer, trust in God, and forgiveness to the minimal standards exemplified by the pagans (MT 5:47; 6:7, 32; 18:17).

Although Gentiles were excluded from the initial missionary outreach of the Twelve, they were not excluded from the reign of God (LK 13:29, MT 8:11). Jesus commended the faith of the centurion who asked him to heal his servant (MT 8:5-10) and of the Canaanite woman who asked him to heal her daughter (MT 15:21-28). The centurion and other soldiers by the cross were the first to confess Jesus as the Son of God after his death (MT 27:54). Clearly being a Gentile was not necessarily an impediment to entering God's reign.

There is another group of people who should be mentioned in this context--the tax collectors. Although they were Jews, they worked for the Roman government and often made a profit through fraud and extortion of their own people. As a result, they were considered on a par with the Gentiles (MT 5:46) and routinely classified with sinners and prostitutes (MK 2:15, MT 21:31, LK 7:34).

And yet, Jesus called a tax collector, Matthew/Levi, to be one of the Twelve (MT 9:9) and, as noted above, he praised the prayer of the tax collector over that of the Pharisee. Tax collectors drew near to listen to Jesus, prompting the parable of the lost sheep (LK 15:1-7). And in one of the most dramatic stories in the gospels, Jesus invited himself to the home of Zacchaeus, prompting his conversion and proclaiming that salvation had come to his house (LK 19:1-10).

Jesus' relationships with Gentiles (and tax collectors) exhibit qualities seen in his other relationships. In contrast to existing custom he welcomed and affirmed anyone who manifested signs of God's reign. In the case of tax collectors (as with Samaritans) he seemed to go out of his way to make this point clear. From a process perspective this confirms his preference for novel contrasts, his inclusive outlook, and the overriding value of the one relationship which harmonized all others.

Jesus and Societal Powers

Jesus lived in a Mediterranean culture dominated by the political, military, and economic power of Rome. Unless a person withdrew into a sectarian existence, there was no way to escape the conditions of societal life imposed by the Romans. Jesus wished neither to escape nor conform. Like everything else, he related life in society to the meaning of God's reign. Everything he did, no matter how "spiritual" or aimed at the internal religious life of Israel, had societal ramifications--and he knew it.

The two most direct episodes illustrating Jesus' relationship to societal powers are the payment of the census tax (MK 12:13-17) and the confrontation with Pilate (JN 18:28-19:16). The former is one in a series of his opponents' ploys to trick Jesus into alienating himself from some of his followers. The issue was less about Jesus' politics than about his religious convictions. Knowing this, he answered in religious terms, subordinating the irritation of paying tax (and its divisive implications) to the primary obligation of satisfying God. Jesus did not exactly avoid the question; he put it (as he did the question of divorce in MK 10:1-12) on the common ground of doing the will of God.

In his discussion with Pilate Jesus embodied the exact opposite of societal power. He was without wealth or friends or influence; he had been betrayed by one of his own; he was accused of a capital crime; and he faced a painful and ignominious death unless he could entice Pilate to spare him. As John portrays him, however, Jesus was unfazed by his apparent predicament. At the deepest level he was in control of the situation, not the other way around. Jesus gave instruction to Pilate and even rescued him from the threatening mob. For Jesus, the most domineering human power is relativized by the reign of God.

From a process perspective these two incidents draw attention to the organic nature of reality. All events are interrelated in one whole, even though they may be separated into distinct categories such as religious-political, personal-social, spiritual-secular with one trying to control the other (which is what happens in a pastoral heresy). Of course, the ultimate determining factor in the process of becoming is each actual event. Despite the influence of powerful systems, general structures, traditional laws, abstract principles, and other formalities, each event finally determines its own actual outcome (which becomes the source of resistance to pastoral heresy). For this reason a process world is not deterministic or fatalistic. It is, however, realistic about the capacity of an individual (or marginal group) to withstand the pressure of an accumulated past and generate a new experience to advance their lives creatively.

From this overview of Jesus' relationships it is possible to draw some general conclusions about the nature and importance of relationships for Jesus and for the church which embodies and continues his mission.

THE MEANING AND IMPORTANCE OF JESUS' RELATIONSHIPS

As described in the previous section, the gospels leave little doubt that the personal life and public ministry of Jesus were completely shaped by his relationship with God. This relationship had absolute importance for him. It encompassed everything else and gave both order and impetus to his life and his relationships with others. If this biblical witness were translated into process terms, Jesus' relationship with God might be called the defining characteristic of his life. In turn, this experience of God-reigning became the common form of the society which emerged from his relationships and continued the experience of him after his death.

Although the importance of the reign of God for Jesus is evident, its precise meaning is more difficult to determine. The concept is complex and ambiguous. Its background stretches deep into Jewish history and is intertwined with both the kingly and prophetic traditions. Its meaning for Jesus becomes more clear when contrasted with what God's reign is not. It is not a political rule, despite its obvious derivation from and historical connection with the monarchy in Israel, especially under King David. Jesus showed little interest in politics as such and avoided the political associations of the title, king.

Jesus' dialogue with Pilate as constructed in John's gospel is the clearest statement about Jesus' apolitical, transcendent notion of kingship and kingdom. Typical of John's dramatic style, he puts this discussion in a highly charged political atmosphere so that Jesus' disavowal of a political kingdom is all the more striking. Jesus' separation of himself from politics does not, of course, mean that his life or message have no political implications. An inclusive theme like the reign of God eventually touches every form of human experience.

The reign of God is not a territory, a holy land ruled by God as in a theocracy. It is universal in scope. All places are sacred to God, and God's reign exists wherever faithful people reside. The reign of God is not simply, or primarily, an image, concept, or formal category for speaking and thinking about God's relationship to the world. It is a concrete experience of God, an experience of one's life in harmony with God's reigning power. This is at the core of Jesus' understanding of God's reign and it entails three essential features: availability, authenticity, and authority.

Availability

As Jesus proclaimed it, the reign of God was a standing invitation, initiated by God, to enter into relationship with God. The invitation was at once free and unrestricted, i.e., there were no prerequisites and it was available to everyone (including Samaritans and Gentiles, as noted above). A person did not have to be from a certain tribe, have a certain level of education, be engaged in certain occupations, fulfill certain duties, or even be in good moral or social standing. At the moment the invitation was extended, all that was required was a personal acceptance.

From a process perspective this is how a relationship with God would be expected to occur. God initiates what is best for each person by seeing, in view of the person's past history of experience (which is culminating in the current moment of becoming), the most creative, fulfilling possibilities for that person. God proposes these possible, relevant aims for a person's becoming but the person must recognize them, claim them, and enact them. When this happens, the person takes God into his or her experience and allows God to reign, at least for that initial moment in that event, as the one who knows the person completely, desires the optimum experience for that person, and makes possible a new moment of becoming.

Jesus' desire must have been that once people began to experience God in this way, they would continue to do so by deepening and extending these initial impulses into the other relationships in their lives. God's reign would become the defining characteristic not only of their individual or religious lives but of the larger world they interacted with and partially determined. In this way (and only in this way from a process perspective) could the reign of God spread throughout the world. It would not be an occasional or flamboyant experience. It would be taken into and made a permanent part of the ongoing structure of reality as people concretized God's will and vision in the actual occasions of their lives.

The role of God as initiator of new experiences means that God is accessible to people in the very events which constitute their lives. For Jesus this was of utmost importance. It meant that people had access to God directly, in their own experience. God didn't have to be brokered or mediated or channeled (the underpinning of pastoral heresy) so long as people recognized that the initiation of each new event was simultaneously an invitation to experience God in their midst, originating, feeling-with, sharing their whole experience. This is how process thought would describe the first feature of God's reign, as Jesus understood and enacted it.

Authenticity

Jesus' invitation to enter God's reign and to experience God-reigning in one's life was a liberating, joyful, enlivening, fulfilling experience. No doubt the free, unconditional quality of this invitation felt like good news to those who were generally burdened by the requirements of religious practice or were judged to be inferior and unworthy of God's blessings because of physical, social, or moral deficiencies. It is not surprising that people in these categories responded positively to Jesus' message--at least at first and as long as it met their needs without making too many demands (LK 4:14-30; 23:18-25).

On the other hand it is unlikely that people would have responded to Jesus if he had only preached an uplifting, feel-good message. They had to experience some real difference in their lives; his words had to be converted into action before the people would convert to Jesus' words.[4] Otherwise Jesus might have been respected as an effective reform preacher, like John the Baptist, but not as the Messiah of Israel or savior of the world.

At the same time it is not surprising that those in charge of religious practices and those responsible for preserving and handing on the teachings of the tradition were cautious, dubious, antagonistic, and eventually determined to eliminate Jesus' influence even if it meant eliminating him. Here especially one must read the gospel accounts carefully. The leadership groups (chief priests, scribes, Pharisees, Sadducees) are cast as closed-minded, hard-hearted opponents of Jesus whose motives are base, whose strategies are clumsy (even if eventually effective), and whose goal is self-preservation.

Whatever the facts really were, the contrast in the reactions of the people and their leaders points to a second characteristic of God's reign as Jesus proclaimed it. It is to be an authentic experience, not an artificial or merely formal activity. From a process perspective this is exactly as it should be. The ultimate, irreducible constituents of reality are actual events. These determine what is finally real and every concept, memory, structure, policy, custom, law, vision, or other abstraction, however important or necessary, must be grounded in them. To do otherwise, to invest ideas or norms with the reality of actual experience, is to commit the fallacy of misplaced concreteness and create the conditions for pastoral heresy.

This is what Jesus opposed in the religious life of his time and what his preaching and enactment of the reign of God was intended to overcome and replace. Instead of a learned conformity to regulations and rituals, he promoted a life-giving openness to the influence of God-reigning. The clearest example of this was Jesus' attitude toward the Sabbath. He certainly respected the religious traditions of his people but he did not allow them to take precedence over the authentic experience of God, especially when it involved love of neighbor (for the two are one). His healings on the Sabbath were not calculated to confront the religious leaders or provoke conflict with them, as seemed to be the case with his cleansing of the Temple and the meals he ate with ritually and socially unclean groups.

Jesus' Sabbath healings were a sign of the presence of God's reign as it manifested itself in the actual circumstances of real people's lives. This reaffirmed the first characteristic of God's reign, its availability to all people in the events of their lives; it expressed the second characteristic, its authenticity; and it led to a third characteristic, the authority of God's reign.

Authority

Although the phrase, reign of God, may have been original with Jesus, the reality behind the phrase was not. The initiating, authentic presence of God in the lives of the people was presupposed by the covenant, the exodus, the holy land, the monarchy, the wisdom, and especially the prophetic tradition of Israel. Prophets spoke for God, on behalf of God, and to some extent as God. They were recognized as having a special relationship with God which the people as a whole did not have but could have, if they brought their lives back into harmony with God by repenting and accepting the prophet's message.

The prophets were not merely speakers; they were also actors. Their actions were often symbolic and embodied the meaning of their message. The prophet's words and deeds went right to the heart of the people's experience and reintroduced into their lives the presence of God and the possibility of God-reigning once again. Their authority was God's authority, manifested in the events and experiences they generated. Prophets appealed to internal evidence, to the divine rightness of what they said and did. They did not seek the approval of human authorities or bring themselves in line with popular understanding.

In a process framework this is both understandable and necessary. If the history of Israel is conceived as an enduring society defined by its relationship with God, then that relationship must be embodied in the actual events which constitute Israel's life; otherwise it is only a nominal identity.   In order to maintain the influence and persuasiveness of this common form, especially in view of competing alternatives, some of the society's events must express the common form more fully than others. To be effective in process terms, this must be more than a generic expression (like reverence for the Torah and the temple) and more than a thematic recollection (of the covenant, the exodus, the exile, the promise of a messiah), important as all these are.

When the common form of any society (like Israel) is embodied in its actual events (the lives of its prophets), those events become symbols of what the society as a whole is (and should be). The validity and authority of these symbols derive from their congruence with the common form of the society which unites and defines all the members. This is essentially an appeal to lived experience, internal to the shared life of the people and constituting the events of their societal life. Thus, through the prophets the people of Israel were brought back into contact with who they really were and knew themselves to be--even though they had forgotten or abandoned that identity (as happens in the case of pastoral heresy).

The picture of a prophet fits the situation of Jesus. He looked to no external human authority to authenticate his teaching or his deeds (JN 5:31-34; 8:12-20). He let his actions speak for themselves (MT 11:2-6), and they spoke of the God who authorized him. He was capable of engaging in rabbinical argument and he often exchanged biblical interpretations with the scribes, but he did not appeal to his debating skills or to approved authorities to verify his message. He appealed to the intrinsic experience available to anyone willing to enter the events he generated and encounter the reigning power of God in them.

Like a typical prophet, Jesus concretized his message with symbolic actions. The most novel and the most controversial was his use of meals to symbolize the inclusiveness of God's reign and the equality of those who participated. These meals, as he actually shared them (MK 2:13-17; LK 19:1-10) and as he depicted them in parables and other teachings (LK 14:7-24), were not about table etiquette. They provided a model for the way of life which should characterize those who have entered God's reign.   They were, at the same time, an initial experience of that way of life and a concrete enactment of that reign. In the last analysis the experience of God's reign was the authority of God's reign.

Based on this assessment of the meaning and importance of Jesus' relationships, it is now possible to describe how his relationality functions as the common form of the church and what this implies for the life of the church. Although the following section concentrates on Jesus and the church, the sequence it describes is typical of the formation of any society in a process worldview. In terms of their actual becoming, neither Jesus nor the church are exceptions to the principles of a dynamic, organic world.

FROM JESUS' RELATIONSHIPS TO THE CHURCH

As portrayed in the gospels, Jesus' life and meaning are revealed through his relationships with other people. His message and its impact are embodied in the interactions and concrete experiences which the gospels narrate rather than in abstract teachings or formal principles, as one might expect from a rabbi, a religious reformer, or a moral teacher. Even John's gospel, which contains the longest didactic sections of the four canonical gospels, grounds these teachings in concrete events as their origin and context.[5]

In process terms Jesus is the center of a network of relationships. As people enter the field of Jesus' relational activity (his environment), they are affected by what defines his life (the reign of God) and they must decide to what degree they will make this defining element their own, i.e., will the common form of his life become the common form of theirs? To the degree they do this, a community begins to form, an expanding network of interconnected relationships intrinsically unified by the common form of Jesus' relationality.

Jesus' relationships (and the resulting environment forming around him) are held together by his overriding relationship with God. This is the source from which he interprets everything; the experience which unifies everything; the environment within which everything takes place for Jesus. In process terms his relationship with God is the common form of all his other relationships and the environment in which they occur. They cannot be understood apart from this context; this context shapes the actual experience of his relationships.

There is an element of novelty in all of Jesus' relationships. Sometimes the novel element defines the relationship, as it does with his disciples, his treatment of women, his inclusion of Samaritans and Gentiles; sometimes the novel element in these relationships is the focal point of his relationship with others, such as his disputes with the chief priests and other religious leaders, or his handling of political questions. From a process perspective Jesus shows a preference for novel contrasts as a stimulus for creatively advancing God's reign.

When challenged to justify the novelties he introduces, Jesus does not appeal to polemical argument or exegetical warrant. He points to his concrete actions, to the people he affects, and to the experience of God he makes possible for them. In short his appeal is internal rather than external; to actual events rather than theoretical principles. From a process perspective this is where verification always lies, not in abstract reasoning or logical deduction but in the actual experience of real events, in what they embody and what they contribute to the next moment of becoming.

The genetic linking of new events with the common form of Jesus' relationships generates a feeling of expectation, a desire for continuation (in process terms this is a society's propositional appeal). The events of Jesus' life originate this feeling but as more events involving more people share the same common form (the ministry of the Twelve, the mission of the seventy), they are added to the series and coalesce into a whole which takes on a life of its own, less dependent on the direct initiation of Jesus and more derivative from the common form of its own existence (which originated with Jesus, of course). Just as Jesus' relationships form an initial environment, so that environment begins to become a church. There is continuity but not exact replication. The common form evolves with and because of new events which take place in the environment the common form defines.

The appeal of this incipient church intensifies as more occasions come under its influence. This intensification is not the result of increasing conformity but of increasing diversity. Each new occasion is a self-creative event, not a clone or replica of preceding events. The more a new occasion contrasts with (differs from) the preceding occasions (for example, Jesus' inclusion of sinners in table fellowship and his disciples' inclusion of Gentiles in the church), the greater the intensification of its appeal and the richer the life of its environment. This in turn increases the likelihood of the environment's endurance as well as the range of its influence.

The intensification and life of this ecclesial environment reaches the point where it can endure as a living community even after his death, indeed perhaps because of his death. By eventually experiencing his death as compatible with the common form of Jesus' relationship to God, the community of his disciples stretches its environment to the limit of its coherence and self-consistency. If it can integrate his apparently self-negating, contradictory death with its common form (as a radically altered experience of his continuing relationality, namely, risen presence), then it should be able to integrate any relational experience that is compatible with its common form. Doing this will require time and effort and may result in unexpected and unwelcome innovation and reconfiguration throughout the ecclesial environment, but it is the only way in a process worldview to perpetuate Jesus' relationality as the common form of the church.

Process ecclesiology requires the church to value novel experiences and seek their compatibility with its common form. This cannot be done as an exercise of logical rationality, much less as a mandated compliance. It must occur as an aesthetic experience which may appear paradoxical (at best) compared to the demands of rational logic. In addition, it is a task which is never finished because new actual occasions keep testing the coherence of previous syntheses and the compatibility of new additions. Therefore, in order for the church not just to endure but to be vital, it must be creative; it must form relationships which include new contrasting elements brought together compatibly with its common form.

In sum, the relationality of Jesus requires the church to seek novel experience and define itself by its creative ability to harmonize the contrasts this introduces. It is future oriented without dismissing the past; it is trustful of its own experience without isolating itself from the larger world. It gives priority to the actual relationships which constitute its existence at any given moment without conforming slavishly to the pattern of relationships it has inherited. It is on the creative edge of God's advance with the world and does not fear the incarnation as an ongoing event.

To see the church this way and to continually support its creative development demands ecclesial imagination, the ability to envision in new situations how the church may live out Jesus' relationality by incorporating novel contrasts into its established pattern of experience. This is the adventure which the Catholic church has been engaged in since the Second Vatican Council. Consequently, the council's exercise of ecclesial imagination deserves a closer examination as a transition to the meaning of process Catholicism.

Notes

1.   This at any rate is the cautious conclusion of John Meier in *A Marginal Jew: Rethinking the Historical Jesus*, vol. 2 (New York: Doubleday, 1994) 237-239.

2.   Pope John Paul II has noted and itemized the social iconoclasm of Jesus in this regard in his reflections on the role of women. See *On the Dignity and Vocation of Women* (Washington, DC: USCC Office of Publications, 1988) 47-64.

3.   The exclusion of women from the Twelve is also typically connected with the issue of women's ordination but strictly speaking the two are not the same. At least it may be argued that the sacrament of orders is not derived directly from the role and mission of the Twelve as such but from the general mission of Jesus and the continuation of that mission by the church under the guidance of the Holy Spirit.

4.   In this respect John Meier's contention seems correct that something like the physical healings or "miracles" reported in the gospels must have occurred. See Meier, *A Marginal Jew*, 617-645.

5.   For an analysis of this interplay between event and interpretation in John's gospel, see Robert L. Kinast, *If Only You Recognized God's Gift* (Grand Rapids, MI: Wm. B. Eerdmans Publishing Co.) 1993.

Chapter 5

The Conversion of the Church: The Ecclesial Imagination of Vatican II

The Second Vatican Council was a conversion experience for the Catholic church. It was not a conversion from immorality to morality, or from doctrinal heresy to orthodoxy but from one vision of the church to another. The primary means for effecting this conversion was an exercise of ecclesial imagination. Rather than endorse the authoritative, scholastic treatise on the church it was given at its opening session, the council chose to turn to Scripture and its plenitude of images, symbols, and analogies to let the mystery of the church emerge in as many ways as possible. While this approach is found in all the documents of Vatican II, it is especially evident in the two major ecclesial texts, The Dogmatic Constitution on the Church and The Pastoral Constitution on the Church in the Modern World.

In order to grasp the sense of the council's ecclesiology, it is essential to return to the documents themselves, for they have a privileged place in the post-conciliar church as the permanent, public record of Vatican II.[1] Of course, the documents of Vatican II, like all texts, are necessarily interpreted from a particular vantage point and with specific interests. In this chapter the vantage point is process thought (chapters two and three) and Jesus' relationality (chapter four) with the specific interest of finding new ground for a Catholic ecclesiology (process Catholicism) to counteract contemporary pastoral heresies (chapter one). From this perspective what do the ecclesial documents of Vatican II have to say?[2]

DOGMATIC CONSTITUTION ON THE CHURCH

The Mystery of the Church

In the opening paragraph of the Constitution the council describes the church as a sacrament, "a sign and instrument...of communion with God and of the unity of the entire human race..." (no. 1). This image links the church essentially and simultaneously with God and all people. In addition, the council says that the motive behind the document is the increasing social, technical, and cultural bonds which are drawing people ever more closely into relationship. In this way a pattern of relational images is established from the very outset.

The council explores the church's relationship with God in terms of the Trinity (nos. 2-4), itself a preeminent relational symbol in Christian theology. The mystery of the church originates in this relationship. The church is embedded in God's primordial design; it has been part of God's relationship with humankind from the beginning of history. As God worked out this relationship in history, the people of Israel played an irreplaceable role. This establishes a unique relationship between the church and the Jewish people which the council spells out in its Declaration on Non-Christian Religions.[3]

Vatican II explicitly declares that "the inner nature of the church is now made known to us in various images," which it goes on to list (no. 6). These images are taken from and are reminders of the multiple relationships people have with one another, with nature, and with God. They culminate in the powerful image of Jesus mystically constituting his body (in process terms, his society or ecclesial environment) out of those who are called from every nation (no. 7).

This mysterious, mystical, spiritual communion of the church is not a disembodied, ahistorical reality. It is always a structured, visible, earthly reality. Holding these two images together is one of the primary tasks of the council's ecclesiology. They "are not to be thought of as two realities. On the contrary, they form one complex reality comprising a human and a divine element" (no. 8). The analogy for this relationship is the incarnation itself. As human nature serves the divine Word by being inseparably united to it, so the structure of the church serves the Spirit of Christ in the work of vivifying and building up the body.

The first chapter of the Constitution on the Church is steeped in relational images which situate the church in relation to the Trinity, creation, history, and all people. The only deviation from this outlook is an occasional reference to the church as an exile in this world (no. 6), a pilgrim in a strange land (no. 7), a stranger in a foreign land (no. 8). These images, prominent in pre-conciliar thought, suggest a split in the relationship between this world and the next. This in turn can weaken the relationality so richly and consistently described and subtly open the way for the type of pastoral heresies mentioned in chapter one.

The People of God

In chapter two the council invokes its most popular image for the church, the People of God. This picks up the theme of the church as a visible society presented at the end of chapter one and concretizes it by asserting that God does not want to save human beings as individuals without any bond between them but as a people (no. 9). In this way the council accents the social, historical character of salvation and turns its attention to the relationship of Jesus and his followers which constitutes the new people of God, the church.

This relationship is spelled out through the images of priest, prophet, and king (or pastor, leader). In each area Jesus establishes a real relationship with all the members of his body. Even though their respective roles may differ, the members of the church always remain in mutual relation to each other through Jesus. In explaining this, however, the council struggles to maintain its sense of mutuality in the face of traditional claims from a more one-sided ecclesiology. This struggle is most evident in the council's description of the church's priestly role.

The council observes, with Pope Pius XII, that the common priesthood of the faithful and the ministerial or hierarchical priesthood of the ordained differ from each other essentially and not only in degree (no. 10). Nonetheless, they are "interrelated; each in its own way shares in the one priesthood of Christ." This is the main point the council wants to make; even grammatically it is the substantive clause while the reference to essential difference is a subordinate clause. But the language of essential difference conflicts with the sense of a shared, mutual relationship; it suggests two kinds of priesthood and, given the history of clergy-lay relations, the pastoral heresy of subordinating the laity to the clergy.

Regarding the prophetic role of the church (no. 12), the council affirms that the whole body of the faithful cannot err in matters of faith because they have a supernatural sense of the faith given to them by the Spirit of truth. This image is offset by the fact that they are to be guided by and obey the episcopal magisterium as they adhere to the faith, penetrate it with right judgment, and apply it in daily life. This description of harmonious cooperation belies the ambiguity and potential conflict (even pastoral heresy) in this relationship when differences of interpretation arise, as they did soon after the council when Pope Paul VI issued his teaching on artificial contraception.

The kingly (or pastoral) role of the church (no. 13) means that the faithful are spread everywhere in the world and at the same time are in communion with each other in the holy Spirit. The council's understanding of communion is best expressed in its account of the catholicity of the church. "In virtue of this catholicity, each part contributes its own gifts to other parts and to the entire church, so that the whole and each of the parts are strengthened by the common sharing of all things and by the common effort to achieve fullness in unity" (no. 13).

This type of interaction between the whole and its parts resonates with Joseph Bracken's account of a Whiteheadian society (chapter three) and is what a relational image of church entails. In this section and throughout the second chapter, this is the orientation which the council takes. It is more interested in identifying and affirming connections than in asserting distinctions and separations, although the remnants of a less relational ecclesiology intrude here and there.

Hierarchical Structure

In discussing the hierarchical structure of the church in chapter three, the council concentrates on the relationship between the bishops and the pope,[4] using the image of collegiality to describe this relationship. Episcopal collegiality is rooted in Jesus' establishment of the Twelve as a college (or permanent assembly, no. 19) with Peter as the head. Viewed in this way, the hierarchical structure of the church is a link with its historical origins; it is an enduring sign of the church's relationship with the Twelve and through them with Jesus.

When the council turns to the actual interaction of bishops and pope, it struggles for consistent relational language. Whereas the pope has full, supreme, and universal power over the whole church and can exercise it unhindered (i.e., without approval of the bishops), the bishops have supreme and full authority over the universal church but can only exercise it with the agreement of the pope. Not only does this formulation omit any mention of the supernatural sense of the faith and the infallibility of the rest of the faithful mentioned in no. 12, it expresses less than the fully reciprocal relationship implied by the image of collegiality when viewed from a process perspective. It says that the pope can function without the approval of the bishops but the bishops cannot function without the approval of the pope. He embodies in his office all that is proper to the college of bishops but the college of bishops does not, as such, embody what is proper to its head, the pope.[5]

The council returns to a more relational image in describing the bishop's priestly role by depicting the local church as a "community of the altar" united with the bishop in celebrating its liturgical life (no. 26). As it elaborates this role, however, the council reverts to one-sided language, speaking of the bishop as imparting the power of God and regulating and controlling the conferral of the sacraments. There is no mention of what the bishop receives from the people or how these functions are exercised collegially with them.

This one-sided approach is even more explicit in the pastoral role where bishops govern their particular churches by their counsels, persuasion, and example as well as the authority and sacred power of their office (no. 27). The council makes it clear that bishops have this authority in their own right as bishops and not as delegates of the pope. This was a much needed corrective to a widespread misunderstanding in the church prior to Vatican II but it does not advance the relational bond between bishops and their dioceses very much.

Even though the council's main preoccupation in this chapter is a relational issue--the collegiality between bishops and pope--its treatment of the hierarchy has a classic, pre-conciliar flavor. The nature of the hierarchy is viewed as internal to itself and fully constituted by Jesus' relationship to the Twelve alone. This results in a closed relationship which can lead to pastoral heresy rather than a mutually constituting, reciprocal relationship which can overcome it.

The Laity

The laity, discussed in chapter four of the Constitution, are defined by a very special relationship which is expressed through the image of secularity. As baptized members of Christ's body, the laity share as fully in the life of the church as clergy and religious, and yet "it is the special vocation of the laity to seek the kingdom of God by engaging in temporal affairs and directing them according to God's will" (no. 31). This is the secular activity to which the council subsequently devoted an entire document, the Decree on the Lay Apostolate, and it underlies much of what Vatican II had to say in the Constitution on the Church in the Modern World.[6]

It is the relationship with the secular world which distinguishes the laity from the clergy and religious in the council's view. However, the council is at pains to insist that the laity's secular vocation is not a secondary or inferior calling, nor does it lessen their status in the church or their relationship with clergy and religious. Invoking the image of the Body of Christ, the council asserts that all the faithful enjoy "a true equality with regard to the dignity and the activity which they share in the building up of the Body of Christ" (no. 32). Distinctions within the body involve union, for "the pastors and the other faithful are joined together by a close relationship."

The discussion of the laity's participation in the threefold ministry of Jesus is dominated by their secular character. The laity exercise their priesthood by offering the spiritual sacrifices of their daily lives in the world along with the eucharistic body of the Lord. The laity exercise their prophetic role through evangelization and draw upon their sense of the faith to give witness in the world, especially as married couples. The laity exercise their kingly role by recognizing the inherent value of nature and ordering the whole of creation to God, especially through their secular competence and activity.

When the council relates this secular character of the laity to the life and structure of the church, it is less successful in maintaining a reciprocal, interactive point of view. The laity should recognize the difference between the rights and duties they have as members of the church and as members of society (no. 36). They are expected to guide secular activity by a Christian conscience, but there is no hint that secular experience, independent of the church, might contribute to the formation of a Christian conscience (just as secular appreciation for the dignity and freedom of each person helped develop the church's doctrine of religious liberty, set forth in the Declaration on Religious Liberty, nos. 1-8).

Likewise the laity have a right to receive the spiritual goods of the church from the clergy (no. 37) but there is no acknowledgment of what the laity might contribute in return. Even when the council says the laity have a right to make their needs and desires known, it is to the clergy, not to one another or the church as a whole. When they share their opinion on things which pertain to the church, they are to do so through established channels and abide by the decisions of the clergy, an exhortation couched in the forceful image of Jesus' obedience to his Father. All of these counsels feed the separatist attitude underlying pastoral heresy.

On the other hand, the council speaks of a "familiar relationship between the laity and the pastors" (no. 37) which has mutual benefits. The laity's sense of responsibility is strengthened, their zeal is encouraged, and their strength is added to the clergy while the clergy make clearer and more appropriate judgments with the help of the laity's experience. This type of reciprocal relationship is probably what most council members envisioned, even if their language is not always consistent with that vision.

Call to Holiness

Before discussing the vowed religious life (which completes the major categories of church membership--hierarchy, laity, and religious), Vatican II reflects on the call to holiness addressed to all the members of the church in the circumstances of their everyday lives. For example, the ministerial responsibilities of bishops should be their primary means of sanctification just as the apostolic labors of priests should help them attain greater holiness (no. 41). Married couples achieve holiness through their marital relationship and especially through the responsibility of parenting, while widows and single people do the same through their own type of relationship and service in the church.

Workers should rise to a higher sanctity by their everyday work which helps their fellow citizens and imitates the labor of Jesus. The poor, the sick, and the persecuted have a special relationship to the suffering savior if they actively unite their condition to his. Although the ordering of these groups reflects a hierarchy-first approach, the overall intent is to stress that "all Christians, in the conditions, duties and circumstances of their lives" (no. 41) are called to holiness. In the council's view holiness is an encompassing image within which the interrelationships of the church are clearly displayed.

Religious

When the council turns its attention to the vowed religious life, a topic it also took up in a separate document[7], it uses an extended image: "a wonderful and wide-spreading tree has sprung up in the field of the Lord from the God-given seed, branching out into various forms of religious life lived in solitude or in community" (no. 43). It is clear that the council wants to stress the unity and interrelationship of the diverse manifestations of religious life. Moreover, it situates religious life not as a middle way between clerical and lay conditions (and separate from them) but as a form of life compatible with clerical and lay conditions and therefore integrated with them.

Discussion of the three evangelical counsels (no. 44) makes it clear that the purpose of these vows is to unite those who take them to the church as a whole, not to separate them from or elevate them above the church—the mentality which fosters pastoral heresy. In the council's view, religious are not set over against the rest of the church but in its midst as a sign of what all Christians are called to be.

Pilgrim Church

Chapter seven takes up one of the favorite images of the Vatican II era-- the church as a pilgrim people. It broadens the relationality of the church beyond the association of members in this world to the communion of saints in heaven--another time-honored church image.[8] This relationship is a reminder of the ultimate destiny of all people and of the uninterrupted union between the living and the dead. Those in heaven strengthen the holiness of the church, add to the nobility of worship, and intercede for those on earth while the latter honor the memory of the dead, draw inspiration from their lives, and deepen their union with Christ. The liturgy provides the supreme experience of this interrelationship and a safeguard against distorted practices honoring the saints. Whatever one may think of the theology or the imagery underlying this chapter of the Constitution, it is clear that for the council the relationality of the church is not confined to this life.

Mary

Almost as important as any specific assertion about Mary is the location of this chapter within the Constitution on the Church. This by itself signals the inherent relationship of Mary and the church. A separate document might have given the mistaken impression that Mary is outside the church, on her own, whereas it is the very intimacy of Mary's relationship with Jesus that explains why she is "also intimately united to the church" (no. 63). Describing this special relationship to Christ and to the church is a fitting conclusion to the council's relational ecclesiology, and a reminder of the perspective which counteracts pastoral heresy.[9]

Summary

It is clear from this review of the Constitution on the Church that Vatican II makes ample use of relational language and imagery to describe the nature of the church. It portrays each relationship as tied to the others and all relationships as tied to the Trinitarian life at the origin of all things. Taken together, its many images and its emphasis on relationships shape the council's ecclesial imagination.

This imagination coincides with the main features of a Whiteheadian society as described in chapter three. The church is a network of multiple relationships, each with its own distinctiveness and integrity. The multiple relationships which constitute the church are unified by their relationship to and participation in the threefold role of Jesus as priest, prophet, and king. This complex image serves as the council's equivalent to the common form of the church. This common form is not just a relationship to Jesus in general but to Jesus' relationality, to his concrete, dynamic way of relating to people through these roles. In a process world the empirical experience is always the norm for abstract, theoretical, and generic descriptions. An ideal is as real as the experience it rests upon.

Not surprisingly the council had some difficulty in maintaining this relational point of view consistently when it discussed traditional topics such as the power of the pope vis-à-vis the bishops, the essential difference between the ministerial and common priesthood, and the exercise of the laity's supernatural sense of the faith in relation to the episcopal magisterium, areas where pastoral heresy has customarily arisen.

Also, the interplay of the church's multiple relationships is described in somewhat ideal or harmonious terms, glossing over historical and contemporary conflicts. However, the vision of inclusiveness is obvious and it is described in aesthetic terms that are meant to inspire, enliven, and stimulate. In this respect Vatican II's ecclesial imagination has an appealing quality, inviting church members to make this vision of the church come alive in the real circumstances of the modern world. The council itself addressed this challenge in its second major document on the church. A review of this document will display Vatican II's ecclesial imagination more fully.

PASTORAL CONSTITUTION ON THE CHURCH IN THE MODERN WORLD

At the outset of this document the council uses an inclusive image to clarify what it means by the term *world*: "the entire human family seen in its total environment. It is the world as the theatre of human history..." (no. 2). This statement corrects a one-sided, negative view of the world, prevalent before Vatican II, and replaces it with a holistic, affirming image--clearly a better basis for developing a mutual relationship.[10]

The church's contribution to this relationship, and to the world, is expressed with an image made popular by Pope John XXIII: to read the signs of the times in the light of Christ and to guide people to "solutions that are fully human" (no. 11).

As the council reads the signs of the times, they are a bundle of contrasts: an abundance of resources over against extreme poverty; a keen sense of human freedom versus new forms of slavery; a growing sense of unity and mutual interdependence in essential solidarity along with bitter opposition among groups (no. 4). This description recognizes the complex and dynamic character of modern life and dismisses simplistic or easy solutions—as befits a comprehensive, relational view of life.

The council's main conclusion from this survey is that there is a growing imbalance in relationships: among individuals, within families, between racial and social classes, economically poor and wealthy nations, women and men, workers and employers (no. 9). In short, the Introduction focuses on relational problems in the modern world and seeks to alleviate them through the church's own relationship to that same world. This is a portrait of intersecting fields of activity in a dynamic worldview.

Part One

Part One of the Pastoral Constitution consists of four chapters. The first discusses the dignity of the human person which is grounded in the fact that all people are made in God's image and likeness. This biblical doctrine establishes the social nature of human beings, exemplified by the partnership of man and woman, and leads to the firm conclusion that if people do not "enter into relationships with others, they can neither live nor develop their gifts" (no. 12). The greatest obstacle to this relational existence is sin which has upset the relationship with God, other people, and nature (no. 13).[11] The antidote is Christ who has "united himself with each individual" and "fully reveals humanity to itself" (no. 22).

Chapter two discusses the community of all people, an overtly relational theme which reflects the organic quality of a process worldview. It begins by noting favorably "the very great increase in mutual interdependence between people" (no. 23). The council attributes this largely to advances in technology but it is more interested in a deeper level of personal fellowship, fostered by dialogue which calls for "mutual respect for each one's full spiritual dignity." Summarizing recent papal social teaching, the council uses the image of family to express how people are "coming to rely more and more on each other" (no. 24) and are interdependent with society (no. 25).

As a result, no one can "indulge in a merely individualistic morality" (no. 30) and act as if their personal choices do not entail a social obligation. On the contrary, "the more closely the world comes together, the more widely do people's obligations transcend particular groups and extend to the whole world." The ideal of community which the council advocates is one where people may participate as fully as possible (no. 31) in imitation of Jesus who "sanctified those human ties, above all family ties, which are the basis of social structures" (no. 32).

The third chapter discusses human activity which in modern times has been creating one single community world-wide (no. 33). In contrast to mere feverish activity for personal gain, the council sees work in a threefold relationship: as a development of natural creation, as a service to others, and as a personal contribution to the fulfillment of God's plan in history (no. 34). Likewise, in relating to the material world, people are to respect its rightful autonomy and cultivate its resources as a sign of God's greatness and mystery (no. 36). By taking this position, the council hopes to offset false opposition between Christianity and science (a kind of secular pastoral heresy) and contribute to a healing of the antagonism that has plagued that relationship in modern times.

As with the discussion of human dignity in chapter one, the council acknowledges that the ideal of human activity is often damaged by sin (no. 37). As a result, human activity must be purified and perfected by the love manifested in the cross and resurrection of Christ (no. 38). This love is not reserved for extraordinary events only but is to be exercised above all in the ordinary circumstances of daily life which prepare for God's kingdom. Like the call to holiness, the secular activity of Christians should not diminish their concern for developing the earth but should spur them on to achieve it as a participation in the paschal mystery of Christ (no. 38). Of course, human progress is not to be simply equated with the growth of God's kingdom but "such progress is of vital concern to the kingdom of God, insofar as it can contribute to the better ordering of human society" (no. 39).

Chapter four addresses the heart of the matter--the role of the church in the modern world. From the outset this is described as a mutual relationship (no. 40). It is a mutual relationship because both the church and the world have the same creator and because members of the church are simultaneously members of the world. Both reasons point to an intrinsic rather than an extrinsic relationship, i.e., they pertain to the very constitution of the relationship and not just to its external functioning.

Summarizing the topics of the preceding three chapters, the council cites the church's contribution to individuals (by defending human rights, no. 41), to society (by promoting human community, no. 42), and to human activity (by affirming its religious value, no. 43). Then in a startling reversal from the past, the council also describes what it receives from the modern world (no. 44).

Foremost is a greater understanding of human nature and new avenues of truth opened up by the experience of the past, the progress of science, and the variety of cultures. This enables the church to adapt the gospel so it can be more deeply penetrated, better understood, and more suitably presented (no. 44). The result of all this is a vital contact and exchange between the church and cultures. In essence what the church receives is a more appropriate way to share what it has to give--a rich relational image. At the same time the structure of the church can be enriched by its relationship with the world. This is not because of any deficiency in the constitution of the church (which is divinely given) but because of the church's need to understand its own constitution more deeply, express it better, and adapt it more successfully to modern times.

The council's relational perspective is evident throughout the first part of the Pastoral Constitution. It clearly welcomes interaction with social institutions and concentrates on the mutual benefits from these exchanges. In this document more than in the Constitution on the Church it uses explicit relational terms, such as mutual relationship and interdependence. This is perhaps a sign that the council's thinking became more relational as the sessions progressed. At the end of each chapter the theme is related to some aspect of christology, signaling that the whole life of the church is unified and understood in relation to Jesus as its common form.

In one respect, however, the council's account is somewhat misleading. It describes the exchange between the church and the world as a smooth, harmonious sharing with mutual benefits. In fact, the history of this relationship has been much more dialectical, full of reciprocal criticisms and often accompanied by conflicts and condemnations on both sides. The council insists in several places that this acrimony is not necessary and it greatly understates its own experience when it says "[T]he church itself also recognizes that it has benefited and is still benefiting from the opposition of its enemies and persecutors" (no. 44).

This irenic attitude is understandable, given the purpose of the document (and the council), and it is not to detract from the remarkable positions taken in the first part of the Pastoral Constitution, but it sacrifices (empirical) facts for the sake of artificial harmony, which is not how the aesthetic quality of a process world is achieved. A process ecclesiology appreciates the actual working out of the tensions in a mutual relationship, including those involved in pastoral heresy. The council's willingness to do this becomes more evident in the second half of the Pastoral Constitution.

Part Two

Part Two addresses five of the more urgent problems facing the modern world: marriage and family life, cultural development, economic and social life, politics, and the fostering of peace. These topics do not lend themselves to images so much as analysis. Nonetheless, the council's vision of the church as a network of relationships interacting with one another comes through clearly.

The council begins with <u>marriage and family</u>, the most personal and, as it already said in Part I, no. 12, the most fundamental relationship. The problems which the council addresses are attributed to the economic, social, psychological, and civil climate in which people marry and raise their families (no. 47).[12] In contrast to this climate, the council situates marriage and family life in a threefold relationship: between the spouses, imaged as a partnership of life and love; between the spouses and God; and between the spouses and their children (no. 48).

The model for marriage and family is the relationship of Christ and the church, articulated long ago by St. Paul and used often in the council documents. This model is symbolized in the Catholic tradition by the sacrament of marriage and underlines the theme of mutuality which appears throughout this chapter. In stressing the mutual relationship of spouses, the council tries to offset two mistaken attitudes, deeply entrenched at the time: that the husband is dominant and the wife subordinate, and that married life and holiness are two separate things—key ingredients in pastoral heresies in this area.

In their place the council affirms that wife and husband are in a mutual relationship of equal dignity and that marriage is the way of holiness for spouses. It expands on the last point by including mention of children and their contribution to the lives of parents as well as widows and the role they play. The marital relationship, therefore, is not only mutual, it is also inclusive (although there is no mention of divorced or abandoned spouses in this larger relationship).

When the council turns its attention to the family, it uses the image of "a school for human enrichment" and touches on the father's active presence, the mother's right to social advancement (i.e., to involvement outside the home), the formation of children, the inclusion of different generations, the duties of civil authority, the support of the clergy, and the resources of family-oriented organizations (no. 52). In essence the family is at the center of a network of relationships which define its existence.

Chapter two discusses the development of <u>culture</u>. The council adopts a very inclusive notion of culture, embracing virtually every human activity within the range of creative expression (no. 53). In addition the council proclaims a new age of human history (no. 54) and with it a new humanism which defines persons as "the architects and molders of their community's culture" (no. 55). Part of their responsibility is to be sensitive to the impact of modern developments on established communities and their relationship to their own past (no. 56). In the council's discussions few topics express the relational character of human life more clearly than culture.

Regarding the relationship between the church and culture, the council first describes the church's contribution to culture and then culture's contribution to the church. Because of its faith, the church recognizes in the work of culture a realization of God's original, creative design. This enables the church to affirm the positive values of culture as they unfold (no. 57) and to promote the cultural participation of everyone, especially women (no. 60). In disavowing any control over the legitimate autonomy of culture, however, the council slips into a less relational perspective, affirming with Vatican I that there are two distinct orders of knowledge: faith (which is the church's province) and reason (which is culture's, no. 59). This suggests more of a separation between church and culture than is necessary and signals the dualistic attitude that fosters pastoral heresy.

Maintaining the soft approach it took in Part One, the council acknowledges that "there have been difficulties in the way of harmonizing culture with Christian thought" (no. 62). Nonetheless, these very difficulties (which go unnamed) can stimulate a more precise and deeper understanding of the faith. This occurs when science, history, or philosophy raise new problems for theological reflection or provide resources for pastoral care; when works of literature and art enhance human life, preaching, and worship; when scientific findings are integrated with Christian morality; and when academic learning is coupled with theological study. It is clear that the council envisions lively exchanges and mutual benefits in the relationship between church and culture, although it underplays the conflicts and the difficulty of harmonizing everything aesthetically.

In chapter three the council takes up <u>economic and social life</u> which entails the relationship between individuals and society. The council notes favorably the development of human control over nature which leads to "closer and more developed relationships between individuals, groups, and peoples" (no. 63). The danger is that economic and material concerns can give rise to an economic mentality and preempt the primacy of the human person.

The council's remedy is to reaffirm the proper relationship between human beings and material things (including all forms of wealth). It is not a co-equal relationship. Human beings are "the source, the focus and the aim of all economic and social life" (no. 63). This priority governs the following specific recommendations (which are equally applicable to pastoral heresies): technical progress and a spirit of enterprise are encouraged but they must always be directed to the service of the whole person (no. 64); decisions about economic development should be made by as many people as possible rather than by a few who gain too much economic power (no. 65); individual and social discrimination must be eliminated if economic inequalities are to be addressed (no. 66).

Regarding work and workers, the council reiterates the relational context it presented in Part I, chapter three: human work provides for basic needs, serves other people, and develops God's creation. The overriding economic principle that should regulate questions of labor is the common destination of created goods. This means that each person has a right to possess a sufficient amount of the earth's goods. While the practice of private property is a reasonable way of working out this principle, private property is not an absolute right and does not justify unrestrained acquisition of goods. Rather "private property has a social dimension which is based on the law of the common destination of earthly goods" (no. 71). In economic life as in everything else, human relationships take precedence and the quality of human experience should be the dominant concern.

Chapter four deals with the <u>political community</u>. It is the shortest chapter in this section of the Pastoral Constitution but it contains one of the thorniest problems from a process perspective. The council situates modern political life in relation to cultural, economic, and social developments which "affect the organization of the relations of citizens with each other and with the state" (no. 73). The twin characteristics of modern political life, which the council upholds, are civil rights and participation in public affairs. Both give fuller expression to the relationship of individuals and society.

The thorny problem arises when the council makes a sharp distinction between "the activities of Christians, acting individually or collectively in their own name as citizens guided by the dictates of a christian conscience, and what they do together with their pastors in the name of the church" (no. 76). This distinction has the same dualistic underpinning as all pastoral heresy. Here it reflects the distinction between reason and faith cited in no. 59, except that the council is even more emphatic. "The political community and the church are autonomous and independent of each other in their own fields."

The council's intention is to distance itself from any particular political regime and to renounce any dependence on political favors--a position with relevance for the Declaration on Religious Liberty, especially nos. 10-12. However, it overstates the separation of the church from political life because it overidentifies the church with its hierarchical structure, substituting a part for the whole.[13] It says that Christians acting individually or collectively according to the dictates of their Christian conscience are acting only in their own name as citizens. In order to represent the church, they must act along with the hierarchy, which actually means under the hierarchy's direction as in traditional forms of Catholic Action.

While it is true, as the Constitution on the Church declares, that the hierarchical structure is essential to the nature of the church, it does not follow that the involvement of the hierarchy is required for every church activity to be a properly ecclesial act. Otherwise the hierarchy would constitute the church, not the people of God within which the hierarchy functions. To put it in process terms, this view suggests that the hierarchy is the common form of the church giving its activities their identity and unity rather than the relationality of Jesus which the hierarchical structure serves.

The last chapter addresses the question of peace. Typically the council contrasts the growing unity of nations in the world with the increased threat of destruction from warfare. The antidote is peace, not as the mere absence of war or a balance of power but as the right ordering of things (no. 78). In other words peace is the fruit of right relationships, beginning with the relationships between individual persons. Right relationships occur when people "freely and in a spirit of mutual trust share with one another the riches of their minds and their talents" while respecting and loving one another. This experience is simultaneously a participation in the peace of Christ and the reconciled relationship he established between all people and God.

Speaking more practically, the council advocates the avoidance of war by curbing its savagery, condemning total warfare, and opposing the arms race, especially in the guise of a deterrent to war (nos. 79-81). On the other hand, the council encourages and promotes the kinds of international negotiations and agreements which reduce the prospect of war (no. 82) and bind nations closer to one another. This international perspective is carried over to proposals for establishing an international community which might eliminate injustice and overcome the prejudices and conflicts which lead to war (nos. 83-85).

The overall appeal of the council is for a better relationship between wealthy, powerful nations and dependent, developing nations (no. 86). Christians have a key role to play in bridging this gap, especially if they focus on Christ's relationship with the poor. In this area the council seems less insistent on maintaining the hierarchical definition of church it used in the previous section and speaks of the church making its contribution to peace "both through official channels and through the full and sincere collaboration of all Christians" (no. 89).

The council ends this long document by acknowledging the generality of its proposals and the need for continual development of its recommendations (no. 91), something which the U.S. bishops have done in their major statements on peace and economic justice.[14] More important, the council affirms the necessity of beginning within the church itself where it calls for mutual esteem, reverence, and harmony (no. 92) so that dialogue may occur, which is the agenda of the Catholic Common Ground Project and a key antidote to pastoral heresy. The council hopes that this dialogue will spread to other Christians, other believers, and all people who respect human values so that nobody is excluded. It would be hard to imagine a more relational appeal at the end of such a comprehensive document.

As this survey shows, when the Second Vatican Council spoke of the church and the modern world, it expanded its ecclesial imagination with language that expressed the mutual, interdependent, shared, and inclusive relationships which constitute the church (and typify a Whiteheadian society). On those rare occasions when it spoke of a relationship in more disjunctive, dualistic terms, the description stands out as an exception to the general pattern of thought found in the document.

Reception of the Council

From a process perspective Vatican II's ecclesial imagination was a prophetic restoration of Jesus' relationality as the defining pattern of church life for the future. From other perspectives the council was everything from a colossal mistake which had seriously damaged the church to another of God's periodic shakeups infusing new energy and streamlined procedures into the authoritative, clearly-defined church it was always meant to be. In 1985 Pope John Paul II wanted to assess the impact of the council, so he convened an extraordinary session of the Synod of Bishops to discuss how Vatican II had been implemented worldwide and to promote its continuation in light of new developments in the church and society.

After a month of discussion and sharing of experience, the bishops at the Synod issued their Final Report.[15] In it they unambiguously affirmed the council's value and exercised their own ecclesial imagination by endorsing Vatican II's relational ecclesiology with the image of communion. "The ecclesiology of communion is the central and fundamental idea of the council's documents," the Synod proclaimed (p. 17). Like the council, the bishops at the Synod did not define communion but used it to explain the many relationships which constitute the church (pp. 18-21) and its interaction with the world (pp. 21-24).

The Synod intended the image of communion to be holistic, to embrace contrasting features of the church which might otherwise be separated from one another and even appear to be in conflict: structure and spirit, unity and diversity, doctrinal and pastoral perspectives, universal and particular expressions of church, spiritual renewal and social mission. The potential for conflict in these areas was not hypothetical. In the twenty years after Vatican II there had been sharp disagreements, and even polarization, among church members on these issues (and according to the Catholic Common Ground Project, they have persisted to this day). These differences were often crystallized by the contrasting ecclesial images of the People of God and the Body of Christ.

A People of God ecclesiology, with its democratizing implications, appealed to those who stressed the equality and mutual interaction of all the baptized. A Body of Christ ecclesiology, with its emphasis on order and headship, appealed to those who stressed the hierarchical structure and authority of the church. Both images have biblical and historical warrant and theologically imply each other. The Synod tried to signal this by substituting the image of communion and refusing to "replace a false unilateral vision of the Church as purely hierarchical with a new sociological concept that is also unilateral" (p. 13).

The Synod's attempt only partially succeeded. The image of communion has been widely invoked in discussions about the church since the Synod but its meaning is still largely defined along the lines of either a People of God ecclesiology (stressing the "com-" aspect of communion) or along the lines of a Body of Christ ecclesiology (stressing the "-union" aspect of communion). In 1992 the Congregation for the Doctrine of the Faith intervened and tried to restore the Synod's original intent by sending a letter to all the bishops on the notion of church as communion.[16]

In the letter the Congregation acknowledged that the concept of communion has "a certain prominence" in the documents of Vatican II and is "suitable for expressing the mystery of the church"--not quite the same as the Synod's ringing endorsement that communion is the central and fundamental idea of the council's documents. Nonetheless, the Congregation urged everyone to appreciate more deeply the meaning of communion ecclesiology and to integrate it with the concepts of People of God and Body of Christ (no. 1).

The letter went on to describe what this would mean, affirming simultaneously the church's vertical and horizontal dimensions, the intimate relationship between its visible and invisible communion, the mutual relationship between the pilgrim church on earth and the heavenly church, the mutual interiority between the universal church and particular churches (dioceses), the dual origin of communion in the Eucharist and in the episcopate, and the interplay of unity and plurality.

Needless to say, the Congregation's letter did not end the conflicting interpretations of communion ecclesiology but it did signal two things. First of all, the master image of Vatican II, endorsed by the 1985 Synod, is the reference point for contemporary ecclesial imagination. The church in its relationships is a mysterious communion; the communion of the church is the mystery of its relationships. Second, no image by itself is sufficient to avoid one-sided distortions or to insure holistic, reciprocal, expansive interaction in the church. The meaning of a relational church and the images which express it need to be pondered and played with if they are to function as a practical guide for the life of the church. This is the task of ecclesial imagination and the goal of process Catholicism, to be described in the next chapter.

Notes

1.   One of the major concerns of the 1985 Synod of Bishops, convened by Pope John Paul II to assess the progress of the council's implementation, was to reacquaint Catholics (or acquaint them for the first time) with the documents of Vatican II.   To help accomplish this, the National Pastoral Life Center and I developed a parish adult education program, highlighting the council's teaching on four topics: Living in God's World, Families, Spirituality, and Work. The general series is entitled *Vatican II--Act II* (Collegeville, MN: The Liturgical Press) 1991-1995. On the relevance of Vatican II documents today and how to read them, see Robert L. Kinast, "Vatican II Lives! Foundation for the Future," *Church*, 13 (Summer 1997) 5-9.

2.   All quotations from the documents of Vatican II are taken from the revised translation edited by Austin Flannery, O.P., *Vatican Council II: Constitutions, Decrees, Declarations* (Northport, NY: Costello Publishing Co.) 1996.

3.   From the perspective of process ecclesiology, the key feature of the council's treatment of the Jews in the Declaration on Non-Christian Religions is the recognition of the integrity of Judaism after Christianity. Among religions, Judaism holds pride of place because of its historical ties to the origin of Christianity. This common spiritual heritage should lead to "mutual understanding and appreciation" (no. 4). A reciprocal relationship can exist only if the integrity of the partners is acknowledged and the relationship which the council envisions between the church and other religions is clearly reciprocal.

4.   A fuller description of the office of bishop is found in the Decree on the Pastoral Office of Bishops where this office is discussed according to three specific relationships: bishops and the universal church (chapter one), bishops and the diocese (chapter two), and bishops and one another (chapter three).

5.   The Explanatory Note regarding this point appended to the Constitution reasserts the pope's independence: "The Roman Pontiff undertakes the regulation, encouragement, and approval of the exercise of collegiality as he sees fit" (no. 3). This almost makes collegiality a papal function. The Note tries to restore the collegial character of the relationship between the bishops and the pope by explaining that the condition of "the consent of the head" is meant to "exclude the impression of dependence on something external" (no. 4, emphasis in the original). The prior history of this relationship and the language which expressed it made it very difficult for the council to articulate a new understanding of collegiality.

6.   The Decree on the Lay Apostolate focused primarily on the activity, or apostolate, of the laity rather than a theology or spirituality of lay life. At the same time it gave new impetus to work within the church (nos. 3, 5). This led to new opportunities for service as well as new theological questions which were addressed by the 1987 Synod of Bishops. Following the Synod Pope John Paul II shared his reflections on the topic in the apostolic exhortation, *The Vocation and the Mission*

of the Lay Faithful in the Church and in the World (Washington: USCC Office of Publications), 1988.

7.   The Decree on the Renewal of Religious Life not only called for updating or modernization but recommended that it be done as a creative relating of a community's original charism with the sources of the Christian life and the changing conditions of contemporary life (no. 3). The 1994 Synod on religious life continued this theme in its deliberations and in the recommendations it presented for the pope's reflection which appeared as the apostolic exhortation, *The Consecrated Life* (Washington: USCC Office of Publications) 1996.

8.   For contemporary presentations of the communion of saints, see Robert Ellsberg, *All Saints: Daily Reflections on Saints, Prophets, and Witnesses for Our Time* (New York: The Crossroad Publishing Company) 1998 and Elizabeth A. Johnson, C.S.J., *Friends of God and Prophets: A Feminist Theological Reading of the Communion of Saints* (New York: The Continuum Publishing Group) 1998.

9.   Interest in Mary has grown in recent years partly because of the influence of feminist theology, partly because Mary remains a preeminent example of what it means to follow Jesus. Among other works, see Kathleen Coyle, *Mary in the Christian Tradition from a Contemporary Perspective* (Mystic, CT: Twenty-Third Publications) 1996 and Sally Cuneen, *In Search of Mary: The Woman and the Symbol* (New York: Ballantine Books) 1996.

10.   Another indication of the council's desire to be clear about the meaning of the word *world* occurs in no. 37 of the Constitution, where it specifies the negative sense of the term as "a spirit of vanity and malice," and is careful not to ascribe this meaning to the general use of the word.

11.   Reminiscent of its statement in the Decree on Ecumenism (no. 3), the council acknowledges that believers share some of the responsibility for the existence and spread of the sin of atheism in the modern world (no. 19). In both instances the council shows a desire for a relational connection even when it deals with broken relationships.

12.   The council's discussion of married life had to face the most controversial issue of the time--artificial contraception. Although Pope Paul VI had removed this issue from the council's agenda, reserving the final decision to himself, Vatican II affirmed the role of parental responsibility and based it on the weighing of several real factors: the good of the spouses, the good of their children already born or yet to be born, the signs of the times (i.e., social conditions), their personal situation, the good of family life in general, society, and the church (no. 50). In short, responsible parenthood is a relational decision.

13.   A parallel case to this one-sided, hierarchical perspective is found in the Decree on the Lay Apostolate, no. 24, which restricts the use of the term "Catholic" to those organizations approved by "legitimate ecclesiastical authority."

14.   See National Conference of Catholic Bishops, *The Challenge of Peace* (Washington: USCC Office of Publications) 1983 and ibid., *Economic Justice for All*, 1986.

15. See the Final Report from the 1985 Synod of Bishops (Washington, DC: USCC Office of Publications) 1986. References from this document will be cited in the text.

16. See the Congregation for the Doctrine of the Faith, "Letter to the Bishops of the Catholic Church on Some Aspects of the Church Understood as Communion," *Ecumenical Trends*, 21 (October 1992) 133-134, 141-147.

Chapter 6

The Future of the Church:
Process Catholicism

Process Catholicism is not a new church. It is an imaginative description of the existing Catholic church formulated within a process worldview. It draws upon the general features of process reality, presented in chapter two: its dynamic, organic, empirical, aesthetic, and panentheistic character. It elaborates these features in terms of a Whiteheadian society, described in chapter three, with its multiple relationships, its self-constituting activity, its propositional appeal, its novel contrasts, and its common form.

Process Catholicism centers this philosophical framework on the relationality of Jesus, described in chapter four as the common form of the church unifying and maintaining it as a living society. It draws inspiration and guidance from the ecclesial imagination of Vatican II, summarized in chapter five. And finally it hopes to contribute to the future of the church by stimulating the ecclesial imagination of believers and claiming new ground for overcoming the pastoral heresies which currently afflict the church.

How process Catholicism envisions achieving this last goal is spelled out in the following four points.

Catholicism as an Ecclesial Environment

Process Catholicism imagines the Catholic church as a vast environment eliciting ecclesial experiences which energize and enliven its members rather than being an established institution which preserves and hands on a past heritage. The image of an environment is drawn from nature. In nature an environment is a structured space that is alive and interdependent with the events which occur within it. Organisms and plants and animals flourish in an environment which they have helped structure precisely for their type of flourishing.

Imagining the church as an ecclesial environment draws upon these associations with nature in order to suggest a life-supporting, life-enhancing field of activity. This same awareness is conveyed when people speak of certain environments as conducive to their conversation, learning, work, or prayer. Usually they are referring not just to the physical surroundings but also to the mood, associations, "vibrations" which characterize a particular place and make it more or less life-nourishing. This dynamic, life-oriented character of an environment is what makes it especially appealing as an image for church from a process perspective.

When the church is imagined as such an environment, attention is focused on the relationships and interconnected activity among the members who constitute the church. Accordingly, six church relationships will be used in this chapter to illustrate the meaning of process Catholicism. They are the relationships between men and women, cultural majorities and minorities, members of territorial parishes and small faith communities, clergy and laity, bishops and theologians, Catholics and Protestants. This is how the church appears in a process framework; it is what its members experience it to be.

Focusing on the relationships which constitute the ecclesial environment of Catholicism expresses the dynamic and empirical character of process reality. It favors the way people actually relate rather than the structures (e.g., parochial, hierarchical) or the resources (Bible, sacraments) they use in relating. Imagining the church as an ecclesial environment also honors the organic character of process reality by envisioning how the multiple relationships of the church intersect with and influence one another as a whole rather than concentrating on individual roles (such as those of the laity, clergy, religious, theologians) or elements in isolation (for example, doctrine, mission, spirituality).

Four of the relationships mentioned above involve every member of the church as man or woman, clergy or lay person, member of a cultural majority or minority, Catholic or Protestant. This illustrates the overlapping complexity of an ecclesial environment (and a Whiteheadian society).

While the relationship between bishops and theologians directly involves only a small number of church members, it greatly influences the experience of church life as a whole through the formation of church leaders (both ordained and lay) and the formulation and regulation of the official teaching, preaching, and practice of the church. This illustrates the priority of quality over quantity in a process worldview.

The relationships between the cultural majority and various minorities and between Catholics and Protestants broaden the scope of ecclesiology beyond narrow religious and denominational concerns. This is a reminder that in the organic world of process reality every living society is open to others, and strict lines of separation between one environment and another do not usually conform to reality.

Finally, in each relationship the member who has been historically dominant is mentioned first. This is not only a reminder of the enormous influence of the past (what Whitehead called causal efficacy) on new experience, it also anticipates that the novel element in each relationship involves a challenge to that familiar configuration. This signals a movement toward mutual relationality which is the promise of process Catholicism and the antidote to pastoral heresy.

By imagining the church as an ecclesial environment, process Catholicism counteracts a basic impulse toward pastoral heresy. Its ecclesial imagination is directed to the multiple relationships which constitute the actual experience of the church as an organic whole. This empirical, holistic orientation precludes one member of a relationship from assuming the privilege of determining how the whole relationship should be understood, structured, and carried out. Process Catholicism views every church relationship as a totality with all the members contributing to its definition and realization through their own experience of it. As such, it stands in opposition to dualistic, reductionist, and stereotypical ways of thinking.

A dualistic attitude acknowledges other members of a church relationship, perhaps even appreciatively, but emphasizes the differences between them in such a way that the relationship remains one-sided. This happens when men in the church appreciate and praise women for their femininity, but define it as complementary to their masculinity which remains primary. It also happens when clergy affirm and thank the laity for their contributions to the ministry which remains clergy-centered and clergy-controlled.

A reductionistic attitude also acknowledges the other members of a church relationship but subsumes them under a single issue or principle which is given precedence and in effect eliminates the other's distinctiveness. Thus the European-American cultural majority may acknowledge the value of the diverse customs and rituals of minority groups but only as a cultural expression of the faith as defined and practiced by the European-American majority. Bishops may acknowledge the role of professional theologians to critically examine church teaching and practice but insist that they keep expressions of dissent private in order to maintain a feeling of unity and avoid confusing those less well-informed theologically.

A stereotypical attitude does not really acknowledge other members of a relationship; it caricatures them in a one-sided way that prevents genuine interaction and thereby precludes the relationship. This happens when Catholics acknowledge the historical validity and accomplishments of Protestants but see them as essentially deficient with no worthwhile contribution to make to Catholicism, or when church professionals assume that lay persons are unformed and uninformed about the faith, even in their own proper sphere of activity—secular society.

Process Contribution to Ecclesiology   Process Catholicism is not alone in wanting to counteract tendencies toward dualism, reductionism, and stereotyping—and the pastoral heresies they spawn. What process Catholicism contributes to this common effort is an ecclesial imagination that views Catholicism as a life-oriented environment and concentrates on the actual experience of the many relationships which constitute the church. In this way it hopes to discover new ground for overcoming pastoral heresies and nurturing the life of the church.

A Preferential Option for Novelty

Process Catholicism imagines the church as an ecclesial environment which welcomes and promotes new experiences rather than an environment which restricts and resists novelty. For process Catholicism preference is always given to the quality of experience in the relationships and interrelationships which constitute the life of the church. And the most important factor enhancing the quality of church relationships (and through them life in the ecclesial environment as a whole) is the introduction of novel experiences. This preference for novelty is the opposite of preserving prior experience by reenacting it as conformally as possible—even to the point of excluding anything new. Extreme examples of the latter in the church would be the refusal of some to implement the liturgical changes of Vatican II or the insistence of others on pre-Vatican II doc-trinal formulations as a litmus test of orthodoxy (an example of the peril described by the Catholic Common Ground Project) with the resulting effects on relationships within the liturgy or in religious education, evan-gelization, and ecumenism.

Of course, in a process world every experience exhibits some degree of novelty, if only that it is this (new) event and not an event from the past. It is more accurate, therefore, to say that process Catholicism has a preferen-tial option for novel contrasts. A novel contrast is not just a new experi-ence; it is an experience that has an impact on the previously established order (as Vatican II had on the church as a whole). A novel contrast heightens or intensifies the feeling of belonging to an environment because it calls for a new harmony to accommodate its novelty (for example, litur-gical renewal, ecumenism, lay ministry, small faith communities). The anticipation of this new harmony is energizing, and the achievement of it brings a feeling of satisfaction and value.

The six relationships mentioned above clearly exhibit novel contrasts which have been inspired to one degree or another by Vatican II. A closer look at these contrasts and the role Vatican II played in stimulating them will help clarify the meaning of process Catholicism's preferential option for novelty.

Men and Women

The relationship between men and women is not only the original and fundamental form of human relating (as Vatican II affirmed in the Pastoral Constitution on the Church in the Modern World, no. 12), it is also prior to and more inclusive than relationships in the church. From a process per-spective this makes it an excellent starting point for understanding process Catholicism.

The established order in the Catholic church before Vatican II paralleled that of society at large: men dominated. The male experience was norma-tive in formulating church doctrine, determining church policy, and evalu-ating church practice while an all-male celibate priesthood uniquely rein-forced this pattern (and intersected with the clergy-lay relationship). Within this arrangement, women were respected and rewarded (by men) for carrying out certain functions in the church such as parenting, teaching, health care, charitable works, and a wide variety of supportive activity ranging from secretarial and volunteer work to cleaning altar linens and running ladies' auxiliaries.

The change which has been introduced into the relationship between men and women since Vatican II is that women now claim the integrity of their own experience as self-validating and inherently valuable. Rather than accommodating to men's perceptions of themselves, women have been redefining their identity on the basis of their own experience of themselves as women. This does not mean that women want to act in isolation from or in opposition to men, but it does mean they want a new and different type of relationship with men.

In society the shorthand description for this novel contrast is women's liberation and the assumed goal is women's equality with men. This is misleading if it implies that men are the standard for determining what counts (which is the source of pastoral heresy in this relationship). It could also give the impression that women want to be like men, or even want to be men. Women want no such thing.

What women want is to be treated as women with the same respect which men enjoy as men. This removes maleness as the basis for relating and replaces it with a new relationship which views men and women as essentially whole persons, with neither complementing the deficiencies of the other. Such a novel contrast implies a new way for women and men to relate to one another--out of personal, integral wholeness--something which neither men nor women are accustomed to doing, certainly not in the church.

What role did Vatican II play in redefining the relationship between women and men? Very little, directly. The council did not address the issue of women's liberation or women's roles in the church. It did, however, stress repeatedly the dignity of all human beings and cited women as a prime example of those whose dignity is often systematically violated in civil society (Pastoral Constitution on the Church in the Modern World, nos. 29 and 60). Women in the church took these meager references and in solidarity with their sisters in numerous non-church settings developed from them a full-scale critique of the church and the Christian tradition. As a result, there is now a heightened awareness throughout the church of women's claims and contributions--and with it the potential for a much fuller experience of relationality.

The Cultural Majority and Minorities

The relationship which bears the closest resemblance to that of men and women is the relationship between the cultural majority and various minority groups in the U.S. Catholic church. In essence this means the relationship between European-American Catholics and African-, Latin-,

Asian-, and Native-American Catholics, or more colloquially, between white Catholics and Catholics of color.

The established order in the U.S. Catholic church before Vatican II was dominated by European-American culture. Even though there were sharp differences among some European groups (for example, the Germans and Irish), European-Americans as a whole determined the normative form of Catholic life (akin in this respect to male dominance in the relationship between men and women and often an extension of that dominance, and its accompanying pastoral heresy). Within the prevailing European-American culture, provision was made for ethnic and racial groups to have national parishes or practice their particular customs, especially in the area of devotion, but the overall order for the church remained European-American.

A major change has been introduced into this pattern since Vatican II, primarily by Latin-American and African-American Catholics.[1] Like European-Americans they encompass a variety of cultural traditions but like women, they have claimed validity for their own cultural experience and in the case of Latin-Americans, as with women, their numbers will soon reach the point where they will no longer be a numerical minority. Both groups, in all their diversity, know that the saving truth and power of Jesus come to expression through their own, different cultural heritage.

The code word for the change in this relationship is inculturation, a relatively new term whose meaning is not consistently defined or used by all church groups.[2] Among members of the dominant culture (European-Americans), inculturation usually means translating the gospel from its European-American form into a different cultural idiom or adapting the idioms and customs of other cultures to express a European-American experience of faith. Among members of minority cultures themselves, inculturation means letting the gospel take root and express itself through their own culture without conforming to a predetermined pattern from another culture.

The Second Vatican Council contributed in two ways to a greater appreciation of cultural diversity. In the Pastoral Constitution on the Church in the Modern World (no. 44) and especially in the Decree on Missionary Activity (nos. 10-11) the council affirmed the value of culture and urged missionaries to respect the host culture they visit, learning to let the gospel take root in these endemic settings. Vatican II also demonstrated its appreciation for diverse cultures by opening each conciliar session with liturgy celebrated according to a different rite.

After the council, European and American missionaries developed a new missiology, based on their own pre-conciliar experiments and the council's encouragement. They showed a greater openness to the spiritual values of the host culture rather than assuming stereotypically that it was pagan and inferior to their own; they learned from it rather than being fixated on establishing, or imposing, their teachings and practices and converting native inhabitants to Christianity; and they channeled the fruits of this experience back into their own cultures, expanding forms of prayer and spirituality and promoting the development of small faith communities (a point of intersection between this relationship and the one to be considered next). In all these ways the relational richness of the Catholic church has been increased and intensified, offsetting the cultural biases which can lead to pastoral heresy.

Territorial Parishes and Small Faith Communities

By definition church is a shared experience. A single individual does not constitute a church; only when two or three are gathered in the Lord's name does church come into being. For process thought, as for traditional ecclesiology, the communal experience of church life calls for a corresponding type of structure, and the form it takes greatly determines the quality of church experience.

Before Vatican II the territorial parish was virtually the only form of church life for most Catholics in the U.S. (with the diocese as the canonical context for parishes). Parish organizations were approved and functioned as part of the parish or diocesan system directed by the clergy (a point of intersection with the clergy-laity relationship). In many parts of the U.S., especially in larger cities, the parish was also an ethnic center providing continuity with the family, work, and culture of the parishioners' ancestors and homeland. In these instances the parish was never just an ecclesial environment; it served a much larger arena of social and cultural experience (intersecting with the preceding relationship).

The major change in the parish pattern since Vatican II has been the formation of small communities of faith (complemented by an array of Catholic organizations that do not have and do not seek hierarchical approval). Small faith communities take a variety of forms and serve a variety of purposes. Sometimes they exist as an alternative to the parish; sometimes they supplement it with services and experiences a large territorial parish cannot provide; and sometimes they are a way of reorganizing the parish to make it more personal and efficient.

Vatican II played an important, although general, role in fostering small communities. For the most part its ecclesial focus was either the universal church or the local (diocesan) church. However, in everything the council promoted, it encouraged the quality of personal, meaningful experience and participation in the communal life of the church. The guiding principle of liturgical reform--the full, conscious, and active participation of all the faithful--could also serve as a norm for all the changes Vatican II advocated, including the organization of church life.

The general support of Vatican II for small faith communities has been reinforced by three factors: a perception that large parishes are impersonal and dysfunctional; positive reports about vital, small communities elsewhere, especially in Latin America; and the desire for a sense of personal ownership and participation in the parish church. All these factors have combined to introduce a new form of church organization which intensifies the experience of people relating to one another in the ecclesial environment. This quality of experience generated by small faith communities is a counterforce to the pastoral heresy of acting as if the parish is the sole, or always necessary, form of Catholic community organization.

Bishops and Theologians

The self-validating initiative which characterizes the three previous relationships shows up in a different way in the relationship between bishops and theologians. In the established order prior to Vatican II bishops constituted the sole magisterium of the church. Through ordination they were understood to be endowed with the charism of discerning the truth of God's revelation and they bore the responsibility and authority for defining that revelation and teaching it faithfully. Theologians were expected to explain, and when necessary, defend the magisterium's teachings.

The major change since Vatican II is that theologians operate as a magisterium in their own right. This does not mean they see themselves as a substitute for the episcopal magisterium or seek to eliminate or replace it. The roles of bishop and theologian are complementary (in the same way that women and men complement each other out of their integral wholeness rather than out of a one-sided deficiency). Bishops proclaim the gospel by affirming its authentic meaning for the lives of Christians today. Theologians investigate critically the meaning of the gospel in its origins, history, and contemporary expressions. Bishops utilize the research of theologians in formulating their teachings and ultimately pass judgment on the acceptability and relevance of theological findings for the life of the church. Theologians examine the teachings of the bishops (as well as other sources of the faith) in order to present a relatively adequate and co-herent account of the faith to the church as a whole. The authority of bish-ops resides in their ecclesiastical office and pastoral competence; the authority of theologians resides in their scholarly competence and the per-suasiveness of their proposals for church life.

Vatican II contributed to this new relationship primarily by involving so many theologians in the deliberations of the council. The input of trained scholars from all over the world working side by side with bishops in the supreme exercise of magisterial authority provided a concrete experience of this novel relationship. In addition, the results of their collaboration greatly affected the church at large, both in the final documents of the council (and the post-conciliar commissions set up to implement and con-tinue its work) and in the impact of diverse theological opinions on bishops and theologians alike. Not least, the council endorsed the methods and conclusions of several theologians whose work had been censored in the anti-modernist atmosphere of the church prior to the council. All in all the experience of Vatican II served as a model for the ongoing relationship of bishops and theologians.

Unfortunately, since the council there has been more conflict and tension associated with that model than might have been expected (which is one of the reasons why the Catholic Common Ground Project is needed). In ad-dition, there have been two other unforeseen developments which make the novelty of this relationship even more complex. First of all, the guild of professional theologians in the U.S. includes more and more lay persons, especially women. This represents a significant expansion of the clerical (male) perspective which shaped Catholic theology before Vatican II. Novel contributions to theology from lay, and especially from female, theologians diversify the field of study and prevent the relationship be-tween bishops and theologians from being treated as an exclusively hierar-chical, or clerical, matter. This development also points to the intersection of bishops-theologians with clergy-laity and men-women, the type of inter-action which process thought expects in an ecclesial environment like the Catholic church.

The second development since Vatican II is the shift from individual authorities to collaborative projects. Whereas before Vatican II it was cus-tomary to learn from the theological "giants" whose works defined their field, since the council theology is defined more by projects like ecumen-ism, feminism, liberation theology, postmodernism, missiology, and prac-tical theology. These projects are shaped by a variety of contributors who often work in very different social locations (the margins instead of the center, the community instead of the academy) and therefore make very different assumptions about the purpose and method of theology. As a result of both of these developments, theology is a much more diversified and interconnected field of activity within the common environment of the church, and for this reason it has the potential of making the relationship between theologians and bishops less susceptible to pastoral heresy.

Catholics and Protestants

In one sense the relationship between Catholics and Protestants since Vatican II has been moving in the opposite direction from the relationships previously discussed. Whereas women, cultural minorities, small faith communities, and theologians have been claiming a certain measure of autonomy based on the integrity of their own experience vis-à-vis their primary relational partners (men, the cultural majority, territorial parishes, and bishops), ecumenical participants have been trying to overcome historical divisions which were spurred by claims to autonomy, independence, and the legitimacy of dissent. This shift, therefore, represents an internal contrast to the previous relationships and a different sort of complexity within process Catholicism.

The established order in the Catholic church prior to Vatican II was very clear cut and one-sided. The Catholic church considered itself the true church of Jesus Christ, in possession of the fullness of God's revealed truth and the divinely given means of salvation. By comparison, Protestant denominations were judged to be essentially deficient, i.e., lacking in one or more of the essential elements of the true church (for example, sacraments, canonical scriptures, orthodox beliefs, hierarchical structure). Given this conviction, the Catholic church had nothing to gain by ecumenical involvement. On the contrary, it stood to compromise its integrity, give the false impression that it was deficient in some way, and open the door to religious eclecticism, if not indifference.

The major change which has been introduced into this relationship is the Catholic recognition of Protestant denominations as authentic ecclesial communities (a point of contact with the relationship between territorial parishes and small faith communities within the Catholic church). This means they are communities of salvation precisely as Protestant and as communities; Protestants are saved not in spite of belonging to Protestant churches but because of belonging to them. In effect the Catholic church now relates to Protestant churches in terms of what they are rather than what they are not. As a result, the environment of the Catholic church overlaps and intersects more fully with the multiple environments of Protestant Christianity--a development which heightens the complexity and intensity of experience for process Catholicism and undercuts the assumption upon which ecumenical pastoral heresy is based.

Vatican II, of course, was primarily responsible for the change in the relationship between Catholics and Protestants. The desire for Christian unity was one of Pope John XXIII's explicit motives for convening the council and it defined the style of the council's deliberations, reaffirmed by the presence and unofficial involvement of Protestant observers throughout its proceedings. Although painstaking preconciliar efforts in the field of ecumenism had laid the groundwork, Vatican II quickly went beyond that state of affairs and launched a whole new era.

This ecumenical rapport does not mean, of course, that there are no differences between Protestants and Catholics or that the differences between them are not important and should not be overcome, especially if they prevent the whole church from achieving its fullest experience of unity. The church's ecumenical novelty means that the basis for this relationship is not determined unilaterally (as it was before Vatican II, and as men determined the relationship with women and the cultural majority with minorities). Rather the relationship is more reciprocal, characterized by mutual openness and a willingness to make adjustments for the sake of a richer and more intense experience of church, which in turn would expose more clearly any inclination toward ecumenical pastoral heresy.

Clergy and Laity

The relationship between clergy and laity is at the heart of most Catholics' experience of the church. For the most part, this is the relationship between priests and parishioners in a parish setting. In the U.S. Catholic church the parish remains the primary form of church life for most people, despite the emergence of small faith communities, intentional groups (like Dignity or divorced and remarried Catholics), and specialized settings like hospitals, retirement homes, military bases, or campus churches.

The established order between clergy and laity prior to Vatican II exemplified a dualistic ecclesiology. The clergy were identified with the church, the laity with the world. The two realms were separate and unequal. The church was considered inherently superior and so was service within it. As a result, virtually the only meaning given to the term "vocation" was a call to the priesthood and/or religious life. In this arrangement the priest performed the essential sacramental functions which constituted the church, supervised the teaching of Catholic doctrine, and governed the parish through the power of his office or the force of his personality.

All this, especially the sacramental role, was grounded in the meaning of ordination through which priests were understood to receive the sacred power to do for the laity what they needed but could not do for themselves (forgive sins, celebrate Mass, anoint the sick and dying). This, whether intended or not, created a feeling of dependence on the clergy which carried over to other, non-sacramental aspects of the relationship.

The major change which has been introduced since Vatican II is the increased participation of the laity in all forms of church life, including the spiritual and administrative leadership of parishes. Because of the unexpected and continuing shortage of priests in the U.S., but not only because of this, lay persons (including vowed religious who are not canonically clergy) "pastor" parishes which no longer have a resident priest.[3] While this is the most striking example of lay leadership in the church, it is relatively infrequent compared to the massive involvement of lay persons in every other aspect of church life. Because the majority of these lay persons are women, this suggests the intersection of the clergy-lay relationship with that of women and men, which is typical of the interconnectedness envisioned by process Catholicism.

Vatican II provided the impetus for this development in two ways. First of all, instead of describing the laity exclusively in the pre-conciliar manner as not-ordained, the council stressed positively that the laity are baptized members of the church, endowed with gifts of the Holy Spirit, sharing in the priestly, prophetic, and kingly office of Christ, and entrusted with the mission of the whole Christian people (Constitution on the Church, no. 31).

Second, the council made it explicit that the laity have a right and responsibility to use their gifts in the church as well as in secular life, the primary sphere of lay activity before Vatican II (Decree on the Lay Apostolate, no. 3). Both points implied a more balanced if not reciprocal relationship between clergy and laity, and it did not take the laity in the U.S. long to act on this exhortation, especially when the decline in the number of priests and religious created urgent needs—an indication that the laity were not as dependent or passive as the previous church order had assumed and to a large degree fostered, in effect promoting a form of pastoral heresy.

Process Contributions to Ecclesiology   By claiming a preferential option for novel contrasts, process thought makes two contributions to ecclesiology which help to prevent pastoral heresy. First of all, the preference for novelty orients process Catholicism to new developments in a positive and creative way. It fosters an attitude of openness and engagement with new experiences which is consistent with the attitude displayed by the Second Vatican Council, especially in the Pastoral Constitution on the Church in the Modern World. This attitude is also consistent with the dynamic and aesthetic character of process reality.

The process world is not only constantly becoming, it is also constantly changing. As noted in chapter three, the way a living society like the church endures is to maintain a high level of energy and adaptation. This calls for creative interaction with the elements in its environment. For this reason, process Catholicism respects the many unexpected sources of new experience and vitality in the church. At the same time the inclusion of new experiences and the preservation of established experiences in new forms call for an aesthetic harmony which is alert to the contemporary world, at ease interacting with it, and confident of the outcome. This results in a less prejudicial, defensive mentality and therefore one less prone to pastoral heresy.

The attitude of process Catholicism stands in contrast to a church mentality which is suspicious of the new, hyper-cautious about change, and preoccupied with preserving the past in its familiar, established form. Church people with this attitude tend to view new developments as either a threat to be resisted or an inferior version of what is already known and practiced. In both instances there is little direct engagement with the new which is effectively dismissed in favor of the old. Such an attitude paves the way for pastoral heresy because it forms judgments about people and events in the church without actually experiencing them. Process Catholicism, on the other hand, abides by actual experience and asserts a preferential option for the new events which church members generate.

The second contribution of process Catholicism's preferential option for novelty is that it elevates the theological value of the new and affirms the panentheistic character of process reality. It extols the new not as an act of rebellion against the established order and not just as a change that is faddish or trifling. The promotion of the new in process Catholicism is a recognition that God is the origin and primary recipient of all creative development. It is God who in each moment stimulates the impulse for continued becoming throughout creation, because God wants things to become new. It is also God who receives the finished experience of every self-creative event, because God wants to know (and hopefully enjoy) what those events have become.

In promoting the theological value of the new, process Catholicism resists conforming to the known and established or insisting on these forms of experience as the sole criteria for judging new developments. As a result, it does not presume to know on the basis of the past what the new may include in the present or the future. This attitude also allows process Catholicism to appreciate the novel, and usually unforeseen, advances which have been introduced in the past (e.g., the inclusion of the Gentiles, the gradual recognition of the Trinity, the development of a full sacramental system, the prophetic impulses of religious communities, an incarnational spirituality). Even though these novelties may now be treated as if they were always part of church life and may be safeguarded as eternal elements, process Catholicism is intent on keeping them rooted in their historical, empirical context so they may continue to inspire new developments.

In this way process Catholicism remains in continuity with the dynamics that produced new events in the past. Past novelties do not become obsolete because they endure; they become more valuable because they generate new experiences. The truly new is a continual source of motivation and stimulation. To opt for the continually new is the most appropriate way of preserving the novel elements of the past because they are incorporated into new developments reaching into the future. This appreciation and preference for novel contrasts is one of the distinctive features of process Catholicism and part of the new ground it stakes out for overcoming pastoral heresies.

A Presumption of Compatibility

Process Catholicism imagines a church which presumes that the new experiences introduced into its ecclesial environment are compatible with its identity and meaning rather than assuming the opposite and placing the burden of proof on new events and those who instigate them. This is where process Catholicism's preferential option for novelty logically leads. It does not dismiss the need for assurance that new events are compatible with the meaning of church; it accepts the challenge of showing that they are.

Given the organic character of process reality, the presumption of compatibility is not as gullible or gratuitous as it may initially seem. In a process world new events emerge from preceding events in the context of a shared environment. A certain "genetic connection" is logically and existentially assumed. The possibility of incompatibility arises only because each event is self-creative and as it develops, it draws into its experience elements which are available to it, not all of which are compatible with the common form of its environment.

Whereas process Catholicism gives the benefit of the doubt to new developments, most institutions, including the church, make new developments bear the burden of proof. Usually this means that a new development must show how it fits into the established order without requiring much adjustment on the part of that order or those in charge of it. Even when a change is introduced and accepted, it is treated as if it had been there all along. In the Catholic church this grudging attitude is expressed when people preface an explanation of changes with the phrase, "As the church has always taught."

Presuming the compatibility of new events does not mean that there are no critical tests to be made. However, making these tests in a process framework is complicated by the fact that Whitehead never spelled out criteria for deciding whether a novel element is compatible with the common form of its environment. Nonetheless, from his description of a living society and the role of novelty within it, three general criteria of compatibility may be deduced.

First, there is a *genetic connection* between the new experience and the common form. Whitehead himself used the term "genetic" to signal that the connection between novel experiences and common form was more inherent than simply applying a name or category to the experience, as if merely claiming that a new element is compatible with the meaning of Catholicism makes it so or that the issue is only one of conceptual, logical consistency.[4] A genetic connection exists when the new experience actually derives from the common form (for example, ecumenism as an outgrowth of Jesus' desire for unity) or could derive from it (for example, the formation of small faith communities as harmonious with the way Jesus related to his disciples).

Second, the new experience increases the *degree of relatedness* among members within the environment. This is the aim of every living society and the primary way it survives. The increase is not simply numerical, however; it is an increase in the quality of interaction within the society. A new, compatible element stimulates meaningful connections among the members of the society and enlarges the scope of their experience.

The third criterion of compatibility is an *adaptation of the environment* to the novel element. This may occur in several ways. For example, the language used to describe the life of the church will reflect the new experience, as in the case of gender inclusive and ecumenically sensitive language. The established structure of the church will make room for new developments, as in the case of small faith communities and forms of lay ministry. The absence or neglect of new elements will be more striking than their inclusion, as when women or Hispanics or lay persons are not represented in church groups.

Clearly these are not objective, scientific indicators. They are clues, reflecting the sense of the church as a whole, calling for an aesthetic interpretation (i.e., do these new developments "work" as part of the church?). To concretize these criteria further, consider the novel contrasts in the church relationships described above. Do they manifest these criteria of compatibility?

Genetic Connections

The novel contrast in all six relationships discussed in this chapter is the value and validity which women, cultural minorities, small faith communities, theologians, ecumenical Catholics, and lay persons claim for their own experience rather than having their experience defined for them by the corresponding member of the relationship. This is an example of the authority of experience, referred to in the description of Bernard Lee's work in chapter three.[5] Is this new authority of experience compatible with the role of experience in Jesus' relationality? Is there a genetic link?

As summarized in chapter three, Jesus appealed to his own experience of God as the source of his teaching about God's reign and his enactment of that teaching. This is especially evident in the lengthy dialogues found in John's gospel. Similarly, when questioned about his healings (JN 5: 19-47) or challenged by religious authorities (JN 8: 12-59), Jesus referred to the effects of his teaching and ministry in people's lives, i.e., to their experience. Although physical healings may be the most striking sign to modern readers, hearing the good news that God's favor and way of life was theirs for the taking must have been much more powerful for Jesus' original audience.

In the gospel accounts the validity of Jesus' ministry is presented as self-evident. The events speak for themselves; they require scant explanation or reference to anything more than their obvious benefit in the lives of the people. While this is undoubtedly a literary device intended to discredit those who refused to accept Jesus, it also suggests that the "proof" of Jesus' message is found within the experiences which it generated.

The way Jesus related to specific groups strengthens this sense of genetic connection. Certainly his acceptance of and respect for women and cultural minorities (Samaritans) is evident in the gospel stories. Although it is not an exact parallel with bishops and theologians, Jesus exercised his own teaching authority vis-à-vis the official teachers of the Law without asserting that the Law was useless or completely erroneous. Likewise, even though it does not strictly match the clergy-laity relationship, he claimed authority for purifying the cultic practices of the Temple in Jerusalem although he was not a member of the priestly class.

These indications of a genetic connection between today's authority of experience and Jesus' relationality are strengthened by the example of the Second Vatican Council. Vatican II showed great openness to the value of all people's experience, including atheists (Constitution on the Church in the Modern World, nos. 19-21) and those who choose not to exercise their religious liberty (Declaration on Religious Liberty, no. 2). This attitude stands in contrast to other periods in history when the church acted self-righteously and even violently to make people conform to its established patterns. The positions of the council regarding ecumenism, religious liberty, and non-Christian religions are the clearest examples of this new attitude, as is its guidance for carrying out missionary activity in non-Christian cultures (Decree on Missionary Activity, chapter two).

The entire Constitution on the Church in the Modern World is a testimony to the council's confidence that the solution to modern problems lies within the competence and good will of people, enlightened by the light of Christ. It so completely disavows a dualistic mentality, with its traditional assumption of ecclesiastical superiority, that its occasional lapses into preconciliar thinking stand out as exceptions.

Internally the council inaugurated a new era in clergy-lay relationships by affirming that the gifts (charisms) of the laity are given by the Spirit (not by the hierarchy) and each person is empowered, indeed responsible, to use them. The council also urged all Catholics to adopt a truly ecumenical attitude of understanding and cooperation which it clearly saw as consistent with Jesus' example and intentions.

These references establish a genetic connection between the contemporary authority of experience and the common form of Jesus' relationality. This does not mean that every specific appeal to the authority of experience in each of the relationships is always correct or equally important or automatically acceptable. A genetic connection is, after all, only one criterion of compatibility. It does indicate, however, that in principle the structuring of ecclesial relationships on the basis of mutual respect for the integrity of each member's experience is compatible with the relationality of Jesus.

Increased Relatedness

A second sign of compatibility is the increased relatedness among members of an environment through a transformation of power. Instead of one side defining the whole relationship (the essence of pastoral heresy), both sides define it together. In process terms this represents a shift from a linear to a relational model of power, affecting the organization of the church as a whole. Is this shift compatible with the exercise of power in the relationships of Jesus?

The gospels leave little doubt that Jesus' vision of God's reign entailed a new way of relating which radically redefined the meaning and use of power. This is at the heart of his joyful proclamation that God's reign is available to everyone. It is not a brokered kingdom or a reward for meeting detailed requirements of the Law. The same theme is at the heart of most of his parables which expose and undermine the customary power relations between men and women (LK 18: 1-8), employers and employees (MT 20: 1-16), fathers and wayward children (LK 15: 11-24), Jews and Samaritans (LK 10: 29-37), Jews and Gentiles (MT 21: 33-43), creditors and debtors (MT 18: 21-35), Pharisees and tax collectors (LK 18: 9-14).

Relational power explains the new basis Jesus gave for belonging to his family (MK 3: 31-35); the reason why he counseled his disciples to call no man father, a direct repudiation of the patriarchal way of life; his disturbing practice of subverting typical assumptions by extolling children, women, widows, tax collectors, and foreigners as models of God's reign. Above all it was the point of his meal practice which sought out and included the very people who would be shunned by the established power system.

In opposition to that system Jesus did not advocate anarchy or chaos but a new type of community where people would be accepted as children of God. This did not eliminate differences, as his relationship with his own disciples showed. He accepted their designation of him as teacher and master (JN 13: 13) but he subordinated it to the priority of service and mutual sharing.

Jesus did not establish a structure (in the sense of detailed policies or organization) for his new community, nor did he create a special language for his new revelation (other than the term, reign of God, and the designation of his God as *Abba*). However, his disciples seem to have grasped his intentions and tried to live them out consistently as shown by the (idealistic) descriptions of their community life (Acts 2: 42-47; 4: 32-35), the spontaneous baptisms of the Ethiopian court official (Acts 8: 26-39) and the centurion Cornelius (Acts 10), and especially the admission of Gentiles to the Jewish-Christian movement (Acts 15: 1-29).

Vatican II did not directly address power relationships in the church but it clearly signaled the desire for cooperative interaction and mutual respect, not only among members of the church but also between the church and other institutions. As noted throughout chapter five, its language consistently emphasized the interdependence of groups working together for the benefit of all.

The picture which emerges from this survey goes beyond a general connection to Jesus' relationality. The new authority of experience exemplified in the six relationships is increasing the relatedness in the church (though not without resistance) by erasing the old lines of classification and power and replacing them with more extensive interconnections. For example, women's liberation is also men's liberation, not as the occasion for a counter-movement (male bonding) but as a new experience of what it is to be men in relation to women who define themselves by their own experience. In the end both men and women gain a new orientation and sense of connection, not only with one another but with the world and their God.

Cultural minorities refute the quantitative standard as a viable basis for relating and constructing the church. It doesn't matter how many people belong to which group (with the majority presumably having priority). What matters is how diverse and rich each one's experience can be. This generates an intensity of feeling which has little to do with numbers or quantifiable importance.

Small communities intensify the feeling of being-together and thereby provide a model for larger assemblies of church. As a living example of what the church, in any form, strives to be, small communities give the whole church a different orientation and way of connecting. They help everyone imagine how else they could organize themselves as church.

Theologians expand the freedom of the church by constantly and responsibly calling everything into question, not to be disruptive or make people feel insecure but to prevent church thinking from settling into familiar ruts which abandon creativity. Protestants offer a mirror image to Catholics, sharing the same fundamental beliefs but interpreting and enacting them differently. Lay persons disarm the pretense to clerical power and reconstitute the relationship with clergy on the basis of collaboration and mutuality. Lay persons also bring an enlarged, secular perspective to the church, freeing it to recognize the presence of God permeating all things and dissolving the false responsibility of bringing God into a supposedly secular void.

In sum, all sides learn to experience themselves and others differently when no one presumes to be in control of the relationship. All of this coincides with the gospel depiction of Jesus' relationality and strengthens the impression that these novel developments are compatible with the common form of the church.

Environmental Adaptation

A third sign of compatibility is the adaptation of the environment to new experiences. Ordinarily the indications of environmental adaptation are more observable than those of genetic connection or increased relatedness; for example, ecclesiastical language accommodates to the new experience; church structures change to make room for it; the faithful are struck more by the absence of the new experience than by its presence. Do these kinds of signs accompany the novel elements in the relationships exemplifying process Catholicism?

<u>Accommodation of Language</u> The most obvious examples of language accommodation are the efforts toward gender inclusive expressions and the increase of bilingual publications of church documents and communications in Spanish and English. The heightened sensitivity to gender inclusive language appears not only in ordinary communication but in official pronouncements, guidelines for publishing and public speaking, and even in the translation of biblical and liturgical texts. Similarly the presence and influence of Hispanic Catholics has resulted in increased bilingual publications, although the primary effect has been to make English texts available to Spanish-speaking Catholics rather than motivating English-speaking Catholics to learn Spanish.

A second example of language accommodation is the effort to redefine established terms. Vatican II began this process by clarifying what it meant when it used the terms "world" and "laity" and by speaking of both more positively than had been the case before the council. The new experience of lay-clergy cooperation has occasioned ongoing discussion about the definition of ministry, the criteria for calling someone a pastor, and the appropriateness of terms like lay ministry and pastoral associate. In the same vein, the role of lay persons in the church has prompted discussion about the meaning of lay spirituality and broadened traditional spiritual concerns to include work, sexuality, family, and cultural life.

More subtly, the creation and experience of small faith communities has been a major stimulus in the emergence of "communion ecclesiology," the current term of reference in official documents about the church. Likewise, the theological insights of small communities in Latin America and other countries have encouraged the process of theologizing from experience (commonly referred to as theological reflection). This has greatly expanded what counts as theology and increased the participants in theological dialogue beyond trained theologians and bishops.

The new ecumenical relationship in the church has produced high-level, technical dialogues which concentrate on understanding the terminology and meaning of the dialogue partners, resulting in more nuanced and sensitive communication. The general ecumenical atmosphere in the church has also contributed to a shift from pre-conciliar dogmatic and pious language to a more biblical and personal-witness style of expression, while those in formal training for ministry now use a common pastoral vocabulary and set of assumptions about pastoral care ministry.[6]

All of these accommodations of ecclesiastical language indicate the compatibility of the new experiences in the relationships of the church.

Change of Structure   When new, compatible elements are introduced into the established order of the church, the structure should change to make room for the new experiences. This may be expected at the parish, diocesan, and national levels of church organization as well as in specialized settings such as schools, colleges and universities, seminaries, religious communities, hospitals, organizations, and centers. In the Catholic church this usually means that the new is added to the old rather than replacing it.

The clearest examples of structural adaptation are the offices, departments, staff positions, programs, priorities, and budgets created to address the needs and concerns of women, Hispanics, African-Americans, and small faith communities as well as the goals of ecumenism and the work of the laity in the church.

One of the most highly publicized projects of the National Conference of Catholic Bishop in recent years was the attempt to respond to women's concerns in a pastoral letter (with action recommendations). Although the bishops could not agree on a final text, they pledged to continue the dialogue and to take practical steps to overcome sexism in the church.

Hispanic influence in the U.S. Catholic church was felt immediately after Vatican II with the spread of the Cursillo Movement and Marriage Encounter which in turn stimulated interest in small faith communities. At the same time African-American Catholics were reclaiming their heritage and pressing for proper attention in the church. The U.S. bishops have recently urged an enlarging of church structures to foster collaboration between both groups.[7]

Apart from episcopal structures, there are national organizations to promote the development of small faith communities, lay ministry, and the spirituality and ministry of people who work in secular occupations.[8] More and more, seminary programs admit lay students; guidelines have been developed for handling disputes between theologians and bishops; and ecumenical activity ranges from local ministerial associations to official bilateral dialogues.

Perhaps most indicative of all are the new avenues of expression and communication which allow those who have had little voice before to be heard. In addition to innumerable newsletters, reports, and specialized journals, there are television cable outlets, Internet web pages, and chat rooms for people to express their views and communicate with unprecedented numbers of others. The overall picture since Vatican II shows clear signs of structural adaptation to the new forms of relationship in the church.

Absence Over Presence This is the most difficult sign to judge because it is so impressionistic. It presupposes a heightened awareness of new developments but this very awareness can incline a person to see more than is really present or to exaggerate its absence. Nonetheless, as members of the church have become aware of the roles of women (as women themselves have defined and exercised those roles), it is more noticeable now than in the past if women are excluded from committees, organizations, leadership positions, and church functions. In fact, representative numbers of women are active in almost every area of church life, including positions of leadership and decision making, and increasing numbers of women are preparing themselves professionally for these and additional roles.

Similarly, it is hard to imagine the Catholic church without lay leadership (male and female) in all areas of church life; without ecumenical relationships, even though ecumenism faces varying degrees of enthusiasm and consistency; and without small faith communities of some type.

One area where absence is not more noticeable than presence is professional theology. Few dioceses or individual bishops (much less parishes or pastors) have a staff position for a professionally trained theologian compared to the staff positions for canon lawyers, directors of religious education, and music ministers. There are several reasons for this: all clergy and most full-time church workers have a degree of theological training which probably makes them feel knowledgeable enough; professional theological work is ordinarily practiced as an academic, not a pastoral, discipline; some people consider theology elitist and irrelevant to their practical concerns if not troublesome with its critical questions and unsettling opinions; and finally, more and more people in the church engage in theological reflection based on personal experience. While all this may be true, it does not warrant the absence of well-informed, critical theology in the pastoral life of the church.

This brief sketch indicates that the novel contrasts in ecclesial relationships are compatible with the common form of the church because the ecclesial environment is adapting to them through accommodations in language, changes in structure, and greater awareness of the absence of the new experience than of its presence.

Process Contributions to Ecclesiology   By presuming that new developments are compatible with the common form of the church, process thought makes three contributions to ecclesiology. First of all, it reinforces the positive attitude implied in the preferential option for novelty, as explained in the preceding section. To this attitude it adds an impetus toward creative, constructive theological thinking. When new developments occur, their compatibility is not immediately obvious; it must be sought out. This puts creative intellectual energy to work in a positive way rather than channeling it toward critical (if not skeptical) polemics and defensiveness. The result is a new perspective for viewing the church, its theology and pastoral practice as a whole. From a process point of view the introduction of fresh perspectives, carried by positive, creative reflection, is always a benefit to the life of the church, even if the new development turns out to be incompatible or less fulfilling than originally thought. In the end it is vitality fed by interest that helps the church survive, not the wooden repetition of truths formulated out of experiences which people no longer claim as their own.

Second, by seeking signs of compatibility with the church's common form, process thought keeps new developments, and judgments about them, related to Jesus. He is the common form of the church and his relationality is the reference point for all subsequent developments.   This means that new experiences are related to the Jesus of the gospels more than to any condition of church life at a particular period in history. The intent is not to dismiss the historical development of the church's relationship to Jesus but to counteract ecclesial short-sightedness which might take a recent, or privileged, moment of history as the norm for judging new developments.   There is also an ecumenical benefit to process Catholicism's focus on Jesus' relationality, especially with Christian groups who do not have a highly developed ecclesiology or do not give ecclesiology a high priority

Third, by paying attention to environmental adaptation, process Catholicism honors the sense of the faithful as a real, functioning criterion of ecclesial truth. All the signs indicating compatibility through environmental adaptation reflect the life of the church as a whole, as it is actually experienced by its members, rather than invoking the judgments of church officials or theological experts only. It is true that most Catholic ecclesiologies acknowledge in principle the faithful's sense of the faith but few clarify how it works in practice or give it as much importance as the definitions of the hierarchy or the consensus of theologians. Process Catholicism tries to restore the sense of the faithful to a working principle by relying on signs of compatibility which arise from the practical response of the church as a whole. In this way, and in general by presuming to show the compatibility of new developments in the church, process Catholicism hopes to overcome pastoral heresy and move the church creatively into the future.

The Creative Advance of the Church

Process Catholicism imagines a church committed to creatively advancing into the future, preoccupied with providing stimulating experiences for God rather than preserving the past and keeping God bound to the known. This thrust corresponds to the ultimate goal of process reality—to insure the process of becoming by generating creative, new events. The key to generating such events is the interest (or propositional appeal) which arises with the culmination of current experience—as explained in chapter three.

In a living society like the church interesting propositions typically take the form of test cases or challenges to the existing order and the experience it is based upon. Test cases sharpen the impact and implications of the novel contrasts which are introduced into an established environment. In the ecclesial environment of Catholicism test cases will foster the creative advance of the church—if they are treated as occasions for dialogue and discovery rather than occasions of division, forcing people to take sides and relate polemically. The former is the intent of the Catholic Common Ground Project; the latter is a primary sign of pastoral heresy.

It is not unique to process Catholicism to desire the ongoing, creative development of the church or to want to turn potentially divisive test cases into occasions for creative advance. Whitehead's worldview certainly helps process Catholicism locate these desires in a comprehensive, philosophical understanding of change and the dynamics of becoming, but this is not the most stimulating contribution of process thought to the creative advance of the church. An equally important contribution is the particular insight or perspective it can bring to the cases themselves. This is illustrated by examining from a process perspective the test cases in the six church relationships under consideration.

Ordination of Women

The primary test case in the relationship of women and men is the admission of women to holy orders. In defending the exclusion of women from this sacrament, the official church explanation does not question women's equal dignity with men. On the contrary, it explicitly affirms this principle and tries to show that the exclusion of women from ordination does not contradict or diminish it. Needless to say, the arguments have not been convincing to a large number of Catholics and have prompted the pope to exercise the power of his office to terminate discussion of the topic.[9]

Process theology does not have any new light to shed on the familiar, conflicting arguments concerning Jesus' intentions and the church's tradition on this issue. However, it does have a distinct perspective on one aspect of the debate. Those who uphold the exclusion of women from ordination while affirming their equal dignity with men rely on the classic distinction between being and doing. According to this distinction, women are made in the image of God and share fully in the meaning of being human. This is not contradicted or minimized by the fact that they are not permitted to do everything which men do. A woman's being (and dignity) is established before and apart from anything she does. Just as a man is not less of a human being because he cannot conceive and birth a child, so a woman is not less of a human being because she cannot be ordained.

In a process worldview this classical way of thinking is reversed. One's essence is not a completed reality from which actions flow; it is the capacity or potential for experience which comes into being as one acts. A person's being is determined by what a person becomes, through what a person does. This is Whitehead's ontological principle (referred to in chapter two), and it is at the heart of the dynamic character of process reality. Accordingly, if women are categorically prohibited from performing some of the central actions of the church which require ordination, their being as Christian women is made deficient as a result. In this case women would be less than men because they are not allowed to actualize a capacity which otherwise they are presumed to share with men.

This perspective does not settle the argument about ordination, but it does put the relationship between being and doing (which is also central to the clergy-laity relationship to be considered next) in a new light. And that can generate the kind of interest which process Catholicism seeks to keep the church moving creatively forward on this issue.

Laity in Ministry

As just noted, the distinction between being and doing also appears in the relationship between clergy and laity. Traditionally, ordination has been understood to have an ontological implication. It changes the person (man) into a priest and this is why he is able to perform priestly functions; he does not become a priest by performing priestly functions or acting as if he were a priest. For the same reason it is a long-held tradition that once a man becomes a priest he never ceases "to be" a priest, even if (for whatever reason) he does not perform priestly functions or if he chooses to leave the priesthood or even the church.

Since Vatican II, in the absence of resident priests, designated lay persons are performing more and more of the tasks previously reserved to the clergy (and in some cases performing them more effectively). It is not difficult for parishioners to envision these lay leaders as ordained pastors, but it is difficult for them to imagine how ordination would create an essential difference between them and the people they serve, or between their ontological status prior to ordination and after.

Lay leadership in the absence of a priest also means that whole communities are learning to get along without a priest in their midst. This does not mean they no longer want a priest or prefer their present situation to a parish with a priest, but it does mean they no longer feel as dependent on a priest in order to be a believing, practicing community of faith.

Process Catholicism does not have its own theology of priesthood or an explicit understanding of ordination. However, in addition to its novel understanding of the being-doing relationship, it highlights degrees of difference within the organic whole of the ecclesial environment. Differences of degree are real differences but they do not separate people ontologically or make their actions contingent on a unique, essential property—like the power of ordination.

Consequently in process Catholicism there are real differences between clergy and laity, but the differences are a matter of degree, not of essence. Degrees of difference presuppose a continuum of activities and experiences within the organic whole of the church. The more disjunct the activities are (for example, marriage and celibacy), the greater the degree of difference (for example, in the expression of love). The more similar the activities are (a priest offering Mass and a lay person presiding at Sunday Worship in the Absence of a Priest), the less the degree of difference.

This approach replaces the traditional, clear-cut distinction between priest and lay person with a more complex (and realistic) assessment of church relationships. At the same time, it calls for a greater range of distinctions and classifications among the people of God than just the two categories of clergy and laity. This in turn should stimulate both the imagination and attentiveness of church members in a way that generates creative interest for the future.

Inculturation of the Gospel

The test case in the relationship of cultural groups takes both the being-doing and degrees-of-difference emphases of process thought to a new and more challenging level. Advocates of inculturation maintain that every form of the gospel is inculturated and that no single form is inherently normative for all. This does more than critique the dominance of European-American experience in the U.S. Catholic church. It raises a fundamental question about objective norms for truth and action.

This issue is at the heart of the debate between the modern and post-modern worldviews. Whereas the modern worldview affirms an objective foundation for truth and action (and indeed for reality itself even if it cannot be fully known), the postmodern worldview denies such an objective foundation and affirms instead a multiplicity of interpretations which together form a temporary but relatively adequate consensus about the nature of reality, truth, and action.

Process thought with its emphasis on dynamic self-creation inclines toward postmodernism, although Whitehead himself can hardly be classed a postmodern thinker. He definitely believed in the inherent and coherent intelligibility of creation, but he assumed that only God could grasp it completely. Human knowledge, even aided by divine revelation, can only make approximations--a sentiment reflected in his opinion that "dogma can never be final; it can only be adequate."[10]

The ambivalence of process thought regarding the existence of objective foundations precludes a facile understanding of inculturation and raises challenging questions. If the gospel is always inculturated, is there such a thing as an objective, transcendent gospel free of cultural limitations? If there is, how is it recognized and who is in a position to recognize it? If there is not, then does not the church require the full interplay of all cultural expressions of faith in order to approximate the truth of the gospel? And are not claims to a single, objective meaning of the gospel only disguised attempts to establish one cultural expression as normative for all?

These are provocative questions for the whole church, but they are especially energizing for historically neglected or marginal groups who now claim the authority of their own experience. Of course, these questions should also be energizing for centrist groups who now realize that their experience is not the sole criterion of Christian truth. From the perspective of process Catholicism the postmodern critique should stimulate all cultural groups to share their experience with one another more openly and creatively for the good of the church in the future.

Congregational Catholicism

The orientation of inculturation toward a pluralism of gospel expressions shows up in a special way in the test case which small faith communities pose. When such communities are viewed as an alternative to territorial parishes, they add to the pluralism in the church, loosen uniform control, and represent a possible shift away from the organic ecclesiology of Catholicism toward the more congregational ecclesiology of some Protestant denominations. The last point is the most challenging aspect of this test case.

The concern that small faith communities might turn Catholic ecclesiology in the direction of congregationalism is predicated on the assumption that Catholicism is essentially different from congregationalism. However, as already seen in the lay-clergy issue, there are only differences of degree in a process world. The difference between Catholicism and congregationalism may be quite great, but it is a difference along a continuum, within a whole, not a radical separation.

In addition, the empirical bent of process thought requires that any comparison should be based on an accurate understanding and first-hand experience of both small Catholic communities and congregationalism. Too often this comparison is made as if congregationalism is somehow anti-Christian and to be avoided at all costs, which is hardly fair to congregational churches and certainly not consistent with Vatican II's ecumenical attitude.

More pointedly, process Catholicism recognizes that the development of small faith communities in the Catholic church has taken place within an organic ecclesial environment. There is a genetic link between the Catholic past, Vatican II, and the emergence of small faith communities. Members of such communities are not anti-Catholic and do not seek to become a new, alternative Catholic church. They see themselves living out their Catholicism more fully, more consistently, and more satisfactorily than they can in a large territorial parish.

The experience of small faith communities exemplifies the perspectival view of reality which characterizes process thought. All experience is particular, and each particular experience is a perspective on the whole to which it belongs. As implied in the discussion on inculturation, process

Catholicism welcomes as many perspectives on a complex reality as possible because only an accumulation of viewpoints can yield a relatively adequate sense of the whole. Accordingly, process Catholicism assumes that small faith communities have one perspective on Catholicism; territorial parishes have another. Both contribute to a more complete experience of the Catholic whole. For this reason process Catholicism encourages the development of small faith communities as an important, challenging, and fresh perspective on the meaning of Catholicism. This in turn should stimulate interest for its future and lead to yet undetermined forms of ecclesial organization.

Ecumenical Unity

The other side of pluralism and multiple perspectives on the church is the meaning of unity, the central test case in the new relationship between Catholics and Protestants. It is clear that Christian unity does not mean simply a return to Rome or an eclectic acceptance of anything and everything (which Vatican II called a false irenicism). Beyond that, there is not much consensus about the ultimate meaning of Christian unity. There is agreement, however, that the primary path to unity is through painstaking dialogue with its hyper-concern for clarification, understanding, and agreement (or at least mutual recognition).[11] Along this path differences play an important role because they give people something interesting to talk about rather than repeating what is already well-known, and they call for communication so that people do not remain isolated by their differences.

Process Catholicism does not have its own definition of Christian unity or a plan for achieving it which can solve the struggle of the ecumenical movement, but it does have a perspective on the general meaning of unity and the dynamics which produce it (already described in chapter two). Unity is the harmonizing of diverse elements into the most satisfying whole which those elements in their diversity permit. Unity is always an empirically measured ideal; it is not a substantial "thing" which can be possessed and it does not transcendentally pre-exist the givens which it unites. Like a Whiteheadian society it emerges with and from the particular elements beckoning for unity and it remains dependent on them for its own reality.

Moreover, given the dynamic nature of process reality, Christian unity is an ideal to be achieved anew in every ecumenical situation. Its content, its specific meaning, its success derive from the givens of each situation (including the past history which they sum up). For this reason, the meaning of Christian unity keeps changing as new events occur and history moves along. This is why a return to Rome at the end of the twentieth century is no longer a meaningful ecumenical goal whereas it might have been in the immediate aftermath of the Protestant Reformation. Likewise Christian unity cannot mean a return to the condition of the first Christians described in the Acts of the Apostles (4:32-35) or at some other privileged moment of history. Even if those conditions actually existed in the way they are now imagined, they are real (according to Whitehead's ontological principle) only if contemporary Christians include them in their current experience of becoming.

From the perspective of process Catholicism the pursuit of Christian unity is an enlivening enterprise for the church as long as it is a creative advance toward the possibilities of unity made available by the particular achievements and experiences of the present. In the same vein there is even a value to disunity, as there is to heresy, insofar as it calls into question prior experiences of unity and creates the possibility for a new and perhaps more satisfying experience in the future.

Theological Dissent

The most dramatic and controversial test case in the relationship between theologians and bishops is the public dissent of some theologians from non-infallible teachings of the episcopal magisterium. This has overtones with the disunity experienced in ecumenical relationships and is comparable to the pluralism fostered by inculturation and small faith communities. The dissent of theologians, however, is a special case.

First of all, it is based on demonstrated, scholarly competence; it is not simply a matter of personal disagreement or even conscientious objection. Second, dissent is circumscribed by the condition that it pertains to teachings which do not enjoy the safeguard of infallibility. Of course, most of the teachings of the episcopal magisterium fall into this category. Nonetheless, it makes clear that dissent is not unbridled opposition to everything the episcopal magisterium teaches but is confined to that realm where there is freedom and the possibility of change. Third, because of the ecclesial role of theologians, public dissent is ultimately for the sake of the church as a whole which has a right to the fruits of careful, scholarly inquiry into the faith.[12]

Process Catholicism is especially emphatic about the third point, not simply as it concerns theological dissent in the church but as it pertains to the distinction between public and private events in the very process of becoming. In the dynamic, organic world of process reality there are no strictly, exclusively public or private events. Rather each moment of experience (including the scholarly reflection of theologians) arises from the available world of prior events, gives that world its own distinct subjective form, and makes the fruit of its experience available for new events. The first phase may be likened to the public setting in which events take place; the second to the private creation of a new event; and the third to the return of that self-creative activity to the public from which it came and for which it is destined. However, these phases are all part of an indivisible pattern which characterizes the process of becoming throughout creation.

Applying this basic schema of process reality to the relationship between theologians and bishops, one might say that the ecclesial environment of the church is a public forum which contains the theological achievements of the past and makes them available for future theological reflection. As theologians go about their work, they draw upon these publicly-available ecclesial elements and give them their own distinct, subjective form. Each theologian's experience of doing theology is unique to that person, but the result of the theologian's reflection (what Whitehead would call its superject) belongs in a primordial way to the church as a whole. The church provides the wherewithal for the theologian's reflection and has a claim on the theologian's work as a stimulus for its survival and creative advance.

This claim is even more urgent when a theologian registers dissent. Dissent signals an interesting proposition arising from the theologian's work, a perspective which is at odds with established and familiar understanding. As noted above, in a process world this is more important than immediately determining the truth of the proposition because interest provides the kind of stimulation a living society like the church needs to endure creatively. Far from suppressing dissent or treating it as a purely private matter, process Catholicism appreciates the public character of dissent from start to finish and recognizes the role it can play in contributing to the church's creative advance.

Conclusion

Process Catholicism views the church as an environment of multiple relationships with a preference for novel contrasts which are presumed to be compatible with the identity of the church while stimulating interest for its ongoing, creative advance. These emphases and values constitute a new ground for ecclesiology and therefore a fresh hope for overcoming the pastoral heresies which beset the church. A final assessment of this proposal occupies the last chapter.

Notes

1.   Although in principle Native-American and Asian-American cultures have the same intrinsic value as Hispanic and African-American, their contribution to the U.S. Catholic church as a whole has been limited because of their relatively small numbers and their concentration in relatively few locations of the country. However, for examples of what these cross-cultural experiences can contribute to theology, see Jace Weaver, ed., *Native American Religious Identity: Unforgotten Gods* (Maryknoll, NY: Orbis Books); Jung Young Lee, *Marginality: The Key to Multicultural Theology* (Minneapolis, MN: Fortress Press) 1995; and Peter C. Phan, "Jesus the Christ with an Asian Face," *Theological Studies*, 57 (September 1996) 399-431.

2.   For an overview of the meaning of inculturation, see Aylward Shorter, *Toward a Theology of Inculturation* (Maryknoll, NY: Orbis Books) 1988; J. Peter Schineller, *A Handbook on Inculturation* (Mahwah, NJ: Paulist Press) 1990; and Carl F. Starkloff, "Inculturation and Cultural Systems," *Theological Studies*, 55 (March, June 1994) 66-81, 274-294.

3.   For a comprehensive overview of the role of lay persons and religious in Catholic parish life, see *New Parish Ministries* (New York: National Pastoral Life Center) 1992 and Zeni Fox, *New Ecclesial Ministry: Lay Professionals Serving the Church* (Kansas City, MO: Sheed and Ward) 1997. On the other hand, in a joint 1997 instruction, "Some Questions Regarding Collaboration of the Nonordained Faithful in the Sacred Ministry of Priests," several Vatican offices expressed concern about lay persons "pastoring" churches and being given the designation of "pastor."

4.   For Whitehead's discussion of genetic connections, see *Process and Reality*, 34-35, 89-90, 92.

5.   The notion of the authority of experience, as well as the transformation of power discussed in the next section, are found in Bernard J. Lee, *The Future Church of 140 BCE*, 47-103.

6.   See Robert L. Kinast, "An Ecumenical Consensus in Pastoral Care Training," *Journal of Ecumenical Studies*, 31 (Summer-Fall 1994) 244-255.

7.   See the National Conference of Catholic Bishops, *Reconciled Through Christ: On Reconciliation and Greater Collaboration Between Hispanic American Catholics and African American Catholics* (Washington, DC: USCC Office of Publications) 1997.

8.   Buena Vista is a national organization of small faith communities which publishes a regular newsletter, fosters regional meetings, and holds an annual conference. The National Association for Lay Ministry is a professional organization which promotes the work of full-time ecclesial lay ministers and holds an annual conference. The National Center for the Laity has concentrated on the spirituality of work through its newsletter, pamphlets, and occasional conferences.

9.   This, at any rate, is the interpretation of the pope's apostolic letter by those who agree with it and those who disagree with it.   See Pope John Paul II, "Apostolic Letter on Ordination And Women, *Origins*, 24 (June 9, 1994) 49-52.

10.   See Alfred North Whitehead, *Religion in the Making* (New York: The New American Library, Inc., 1974 edition) 126.

11.   For a thorough discussion of the method used in ecumenical dialogues, see G. R. Evans, *Method in Ecumenical Theology: The Lessons So Far* (Cambridge: Cambridge University Press) 1996.

12.   This right is not acknowledged by the Congregation for the Doctrine of the Faith in its "Instruction on the Ecclesial Vocation of the Theologian," *Origins*, 20 (July 5, 1990) 117-126.   According to that document, dissent is to be handled privately (no. 27) in dialogue only with magisterial authorities (no. 30) and with the hope that a theologian's difficulties will be resolved in favor of the magisterium's teaching.

Chapter 7

The Hope of the Church:
Overcoming Incarnational Cowardice

Process Catholicism is a response to the pastoral heresies which currently confront the Catholic church. A pastoral heresy is a deliberate choice to structure and carry out the practical life of the church erroneously. At the present time the most fundamental error and the most pervasive form of pastoral heresy occurs when one member of a church relationship acts unilaterally to determine how the other members of the relationship should function. This practice is heretical because it contradicts the relationality of Jesus which is at the origin of the church and remains its principle of identity and coherence.

The pastoral heresies which have been identified and discussed in this book are a continuation of an earlier era when the error of a one-sided determination of church relationships was not very obvious. However, since the Second Vatican Council and the reappropriation of the gospel testimony which it inspired, these errors are now more evident, even if they are not called pastoral heresies. In the years since Vatican II there have been persistent attempts to correct these distorted relationships but the problem has not yet been satisfactorily resolved; in fact it has become more acute and threatening.

This situation has given rise to the Catholic Common Ground Project, initiated by the late Cardinal Bernardin. Process Catholicism shares the spirit of that project but takes a different direction in seeking new ground rather than familiar common ground to overcome the "bickering, disparagement and stalemate" which now grip the church. To do this, process Catholicism draws upon Alfred North Whitehead's philosophy of organism as a comprehensive worldview within which the life of the church may be seen and analyzed in a fresh way.

The features of this worldview which process Catholicism finds relevant to ecclesiology have already been elaborated. At this point two final questions must be addressed: what makes process Catholicism Catholic, and does process Catholicism get to the root cause of pastoral heresy?

The first question arises because the typical emphases of Catholic ecclesiology do not show up in process Catholicism. The reason is that process Catholicism is not an ecclesiology in the usual sense. It is not a theoretical exposition of the nature of the church and its essential elements, such as faith and doctrine, sacraments, hierarchical structure, mission, etc. Rather it is a description of the Catholic church as it currently functions from the perspective of a process worldview. In keeping with the empirical character of that worldview, process Catholicism accepts as part of the Catholic church whatever has in fact been included in its historical development. It is as Catholic as the Catholic church actually is. Unlike typical ecclesiologies, it is not interested in putting these elements into a systematic order or ranking them according to priority or using them to compare the Catholic church to other churches and institutions. Process Catholicism is interested in seeing how the elements in the Catholic environment actually work together and what sort of collective experience they generate.

This is what a process worldview can contribute to ecclesiology, not a distinct theological message but a comprehensive understanding of how reality functions. In light of that understanding process Catholicism seeks to determine how the Catholic church functions, how it could function better, and what would be required for this to happen. The results of this inquiry have been laid out in the preceding chapters. In keeping with the organic, relational character of process thought, the focus of attention has been on the relationships which constitute the actual life of the church and the pastoral heresies which prevent the church from achieving its fullest experience of those relationships.

This focus of attention leads to the second question: does process Catholicism get to the root cause of pastoral heresy? Obviously the answer to this question depends on what the root cause is, and that cause is not self-evident. When confronted with a pastoral (or doctrinal) heresy, there is a tendency to attribute motives to the individual or group responsible for the heresy, such as a desire for power or a need to control or some personality deficiency. While it is always possible that this may be the case (though few people who make such a judgment are in a position to know for sure), it would mean that the root cause of pastoral heresy is an individual shortcoming and the solution is to deal with it on an individual basis. My conviction is that something more inherent in the ecclesial environment of the church itself is at the root of pastoral heresy. That something is incarnational cowardice.

Incarnational cowardice is the fear that God, having become human in Jesus, wants to remain human. The fear inspired by this prospect is twofold. On the one hand, it means that God continues to function within the limitations and contingencies of the human condition. This is not the kind of God most church people want or believe in. They expect God to be free of the curtailments and obstacles of human life. This is what it means to be God rather than human, or even superhuman. It is frightening to think of God being permanently incarnate, limited by human circumstances and struggling with people to advance creatively. Such a God seems too involved with the human condition to exercise universal providence over it and guarantee eternal salvation for it. It is much more comforting and inspiring to believe that a transcendent, all-powerful God is ready, able, and willing to make up for human deficiencies and insure that people's best efforts will eventually succeed, perhaps even beyond their wildest hopes.

On the other hand, if God is permanently incarnate and not the independent designer of a plan for human history and the guarantor of its success, then a much greater responsibility falls on each believer to discern and realize God's desires in their own lives, the life of the church, the life of human society, and the world at large. It is indeed frightening to think that God's vision and power are dependent on the quality of experience human beings generate. It is much more comforting and inspiring to assume that there is an exception to the conditions of creation, a protection against the possibility that everything could end in failure, an independent source who will ultimately vindicate all our hopes.

Facing both of these implications tends to make cowards of believers. We feel our own needs and know our own limitations so well that we prefer to dis-incarnate God and rely on a system of intermediaries rather than embrace the incarnation courageously. This is why incarnational cowardice is the root cause of pastoral heresy. It opens the way for some members of the church to fill the presumed void between God and the rest of the church and to determine from this position of privilege how the rest of the church should function.

Process Catholicism confronts both of these implications with a fiercely incarnational stance, rooted in an affirmation of the becoming of God and the interdependence of meaning and experience.

Most Christians affirm the proclamation of John's gospel that "the Word became flesh" (1:14) without giving much thought to what it means to become. Not so, Alfred North Whitehead. The meaning and process of becoming preoccupied his thinking. In his worldview the only God who makes sense, i.e., who is intelligible in terms of the ontological principle, is a God who continually becomes along with the rest of creation. In this respect God's incarnation is not a one-time intervention in the course of history; it is the way God always is, who God always is. At the same time, God's becoming is not like the becoming of any other entity.

As described in chapter two, God takes into the divine experience all the events which occur at the very moment of their completion. This means that God has a comprehensive knowledge (omniscience) of all actual things. More than that, God sees all the possible developments which could emerge from these just-completed events and God ranks or values them according to their potential for realizing the highest values: unity, peace, love, beauty. This is God's providence, a divine anticipation of what created (and creative) life might become, given what it now is.

God does not keep this vision private. Rather God shares it with the world in the form of impulses or attractions offered as persuasively as possible for the free, creative response of creatures. This is God's power: to entice creation toward its own best and most fulfilling experience. It is not domineering or one-sided or unconditioned; God's power is suggestive, reciprocal, and contingent. That may not seem like power in a human sense but it is how God functions in a process world. And God does not know from moment to moment how creation will respond, what sort of new becoming will result. That is for each creature to determine in their own circumstances. God's becoming is an incarnational adventure, for God as well as for creation.

To recognize these divine dynamics at work in Jesus is to bring the universal role of God which encompasses all particular events to a personal and recognizable location in human experience. This is the source of contact with God's fullness for human beings. Not by leaving human experience but by entering more deeply into it do we encounter the living God and discover who we are and yet can be. Far from cowering in the face of the incarnation's implications, process Catholicism embraces the becoming of God with us, for it knows nowhere else to find God.

At the same time process thought recognizes that the becoming of God as well as our experience of God and its implications for ourselves are contingent on the quality of the events we generate. This is true throughout the process world. Nothing is given gratuitously or assured absolutely. Everything depends on the quality of actual events which feed the becoming of all things. Thus there is no separate reality called church, distinct from and unaffected by the actions of its members. Church is the environment which has been formed by the actions of all its members throughout history. This collective history or environment influences the current actions of church members and is in turn modified by those same actions. The becoming of the church is the becoming of its members, and part of the becoming of God.

While this view might incline some to feel a heavy sense of responsibility and obligation, it is intended in the worldview of Whitehead to generate a feeling of excitement, freedom, and creativity. In the theological worldview of process Catholicism this translates into a sense of giving delight to God by shaping the experience of the church as creatively and imaginatively as possible. For in the end whether viewed from the perspective of process philosophy or process Catholicism, the aim of all creation is to serve the becoming of God.

A fragmented, argumentative, power-driven, privilege-seeking, pastorally heretical church doesn't give God much to go on. Process Catholicism hopes to offer more than that by imagining the church as an ecclesial environment constituted by mutual relationships and characterized by novel contrasts which are compatible with the identity of the church and stimulating for future experiences not yet imagined by the church, the world, or even God. In such a church there is neither time nor place for pastoral heresy.

Index

Note: Some entries that appear throughout the book, such as ecclesial imagination and process ecclesiology, are not listed in the index.